Welcome to
Table Talk

Table Talk helps children and adults explore the
Bible together. Each day provides a short family
Bible time which, with your own adaptation, could work for ages 4 to 12. It includes
optional follow on material which takes the passage further for older children. There are
also suggestions for linking **Table Talk** with **XTB** children's notes.

> Who can use
> Table Talk?

Table Talk

A short family Bible time for daily
use. Table Talk takes about five
minutes, maybe at breakfast,
or after an evening meal. Choose
whatever time and place suits you
best as a family. Table Talk includes
a simple discussion starter or
activity that leads into a short
Bible reading. This is followed
by a few questions.

- **Families**
- **One adult with one child**
- **A teenager with a younger
  brother or sister**
- **Children's leaders with their groups**
- **Any other mix that works for you!**

XTB

XTB children's notes help 7-11 year olds to get
into the Bible for themselves. They are based on
the same Bible passages as **Table Talk**.
You will find suggestions for how **XTB** can be
used alongside **Table Talk** on the next page.

In the next three pages you'll find suggestions for how to use Table Talk, along with hints
and tips for adapting it to your own situation. If you've never done anything like this
before, check out our web page for further help (go to www.thegoodbook.co.uk and click
on Daily Reading) or write in for a fact sheet.

THE SMALL PRINT

Table Talk is published by The Good Book Company, 37 Elm Road, New Malden, Surrey, KT3 3HB
Tel: 0845 225 0880. www.thegoodbook.co.uk. Written by Alison Mitchell. email: Alison@thegoodbook.co.uk
Fab pictures by Kirsty McAllister. Bible quotations taken from The Good News Bible.
AUSTRALIA: Distributed by Matthias Media. Tel: (02) 9663 1478; email: info@matthiasmedia.com.au

HOW TO USE
Table Talk

● **Table Talk** is designed to last for up to three mon
How you use it depends on what works for you.
have included 65 full days of material in this issu
plus some more low-key suggestions for another
days (at the back of the book). We would like to
encourage you to work establishing a pattern of
family reading. The first two weeks are the harde

DAY 1
What shall we do?

KEYPOINT
When the people heard Peter's speech, they asked, "What shall we do?" **Read Acts 2v38-39**

Today's passages are:
Table Talk Acts 2v38-39
XTB Acts 2v37-40

Recap: Look again at yesterday's five points from Peter's speech.

When the people heard Peter's speech, they asked, "What shall we do?" **Read Acts 2v38-39**

Peter told them to **repent**. What does that mean? (To repent doesn't just mean saying sorry. It means asking God to help you to **change**, and to do what He says.) What two things did Peter say would happen? (Their sins will be forgiven, they'll be given the gift of the Holy Spirit.)

DO Use the illustration in **Notes for Parents** (on the previous page) to show how Jesus rescues us from our sins.

PRAY Verse 39 means that this promise is for us too—even though we live 2000 years after Peter! Thank God for sending Jesus so that you can be forgiven.

Building up
The apostles had the task of telling others about Jesus. Some of them also wrote the books that make up the New T. But what if they <u>forgot</u> some of what they had seen or heard? Or didn't <u>understand</u> it? **Read John 14v25-26** to see how the Holy Spirit helped them. Thank God for making sure that what the apostles taught and wrote down about Jesus was true and accurate.

● **Table Talk** is based on the same Bible passages as *XTB*, but usually only asks for two or three verses to be read out loud. The full *XTB* passage is listed at the top of each **Table Talk** page. If you are using **Table Talk** with older children, read the full *XTB* passage rather than the shorter version.

● KEYPOINT
This is the main point you should be trying to convey. Don't read this out—it often gives away the end of the story

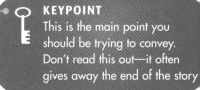

●The main part of **Table Talk** is designed to be suitable for younger children. Building Up includes more difficult questions designed for older children, or those with more Bible knowledge.

As far as possible, if your children are old enough to read the Bible verses for themselves, encourage them to find the answers in the passage and to tell you which verse the answer is in. This will help them to get used to handling the Bible for themselves.

● The **Building Up** section is designed to build on the passage studied in Table Talk (and XTB). Building Up includes some additional questions which reinforce the main teaching point, apply the teaching more directly or follow up any difficult issues raised by the passage.

Linking with *XTB*

The **XTB** children's notes are based on the same passages as **Table Talk**. There are a number of ways in which you can link the two together:
• Children do **XTB** on their own. Parents then follow these up later (see suggestions below).
• A child and adult work through **XTB** together.
• A family uses **Table Talk** together at breakfast. Older children then use **XTB** on their own later.
• You use **Table Talk** on its own, with no link to **XTB**.

FOLLOWING UP XTB

If your child uses **XTB** on their own it can be helpful to ask them later to show you (or tell you) what they've done. Some useful starter questions are:

• Can you tell me what the reading was about?

• Is there anything you didn't understand or want to ask about?

• Did anything surprise you in the reading? Was there anything that would have surprised the people who first saw it or read about it?

• What did you learn about God, Jesus or the Holy Spirit?

• Is there anything you're going to do as a result of reading this passage?

Table Talk is deliberately not too ambitious. Most families find it quite hard to set up a regular pattern of reading the Bible together—and when they do meet, time is often short. So **Table Talk** is designed to be quick and easy to use, needing little in the way of extra materials, apart from pen and paper now and then.

BUT!!

Most families have special times when they **can** be more ambitious, or do have some extra time available. Here are some suggestions for how you can use **Table Talk** as the basis for a special family adventure...

PICNIC

Take Table Talk with you on a family picnic. Thank God for His beautiful Creation.

WALK

Go for a walk together. Stop somewhere with a good view and read Genesis 1v1—2v4.

GETTING TOGETHER

Invite another family for a meal, and to read the Bible together. The children could make a poster based on the passage.

MUSEUM

Visit a museum to see a display from Bible times. Use it to remind yourselves that the Bible tells us about real people and real history.

HOLIDAYS

Set aside a special time each day while on holiday. Choose some unusual places to read the Bible together—on the beach, up a mountain, in a boat... Take some photos to put on your Tale Talk display when you get back from holiday.

You could try one of the special holiday editions of XTB and Table Talk—**Christmas Unpacked, Easter Unscrambled** and **Summer Signposts.**

Have an
adventure!

FOOD!

Eat some food linked with the passage you are studying. For example Manna (biscuits made with honey, Exodus 16v31), Unleavened bread or Honeycomb (Matthew 3v4— but don't try the locusts!)

DISPLAY AREA

We find it easier to remember and understand what we learn when we have something to look at. Make a Table Talk display area, for pictures, Bible verses and prayers. Add to it regularly.

VIDEO

A wide range of Bible videos are available—from simple cartoon stories, to whole Gospels filmed with real life actors. (Your local Christian bookshop should have a range.) Choose one that ties in with the passages you are reading together. ***Note:*** Use the video **in addition** to the Bible passage, not **instead** of it!

PRAYER DIARY

As a special project, make a family prayer diary. Use it to keep a note of things you pray for—and the answers God gives you. This can be a tremendous help to children (and parents!) to learn to trust God in prayer as we see how He answers over time.

Go on—try it!

DRAMA OR PUPPETS

Take time to dramatise a Bible story. Maybe act it out (with costumes if possible) or make some simple puppets to retell the story.

Enough of the introduction, let's get going...

DAYS 1-15
Notes for Parents

THE BOOK OF ACTS

The second half of Acts tells us about Paul's three Missionary Journeys, as he travelled from country to country telling people about Jesus.

In Table Talk we will investigate Paul's second journey, which starts with a crucial council meeting in Jerusalem.

Paul's Missionary Journeys

JERUSALEM COUNCIL

The Jerusalem Council in chapter 15 is central to Acts. As the early church grew, more and more Gentiles (non-Jews) became Christians. The Jewish believers were divided about these Gentiles. Some (like Paul) said that the <u>only</u> way to be right with God is to put your trust in Jesus. Nothing else must be added. But others were saying that the Gentiles must <u>also</u> keep the Jewish law, and be circumcised.

Paul spoke out strongly against this suggestion. It implied that Jesus' death and resurrection were <u>not enough</u> to make us right with God, and that something else needed to be added. Paul knew this was wrong.

Today there are still false teachers who suggest that we have to <u>add</u> something else to the Gospel message. (Maybe about how we pray, what church we attend or even which Bible version we read.) This is always wrong. As Peter put it during the Jerusalem Council:

> **"We believe it is through the grace of our Lord Jesus that we are saved."** Acts 15v11

DAY 1
Adding Up

KEYPOINT
Some people said Gentiles had to keep Jewish rules to be right with God. Paul disagreed!

Today's passages are:
Table Talk: Acts 15v1-2
XTB: Acts 15v1-5

TABLE TALK

Play Hangman to guess the word **Mission**, <u>and/or</u> look up **Mission** in dictionary.

Paul was a Missionary—a man with a mission. His task was to tell other people all about Jesus. He travelled on three lon journeys to do this. We're going to read about his **2nd Missionary Journey**

READ

Everywhere Paul want he told people th the <u>only</u> way to be right with God is to put your trust in **Jesus**. But some peopl were *adding stuff* to the message. **Read Acts 15v1-2**

TALK

Some men from Judea were teaching th new believers. What did they say peopl had to do? (v1) (*Be circumcised.*)

Explain: Circumcision meant having a small piece of skin cut off. It was a sign of being Jewish. These people were saying that Gentiles (non-Jews) had to b circumcised <u>as well as</u> trusting in Jesus.

Did Paul agree? (v2) (*No!*) Where did Paul go? (v2) (*To Jerusalem, to meet th Christians leaders there.*)

PRAY

This disagreement mattered because people were teaching different things about Jesus. Ask God to help you to understand the **truth** about Jesus as yo read the book of Acts together.

Building up

Read **Acts 15v3-5**. As Paul and Barnabas travelled to Jerusalem they told people about the Gentiles becoming Christians. Everyone was very excited. Are <u>you</u> excited about new Christians in your church or family? Thank God for anyone you know who has become a follower of Jesus.

DAY 2
Red Letter Day

KEYPOINT
"It is through the grace of our Lord Jesus that we are saved."
Acts 15v11

Today's passages are:
Table Talk: Acts 15v11 & 31
XTB: Acts 15v6-35

TABLE TALK

Collect some things that came by **post** (e.g. a letter, birthday card, phone bill, catalogue...) Why was each one sent?

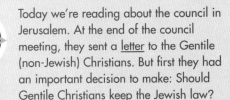

READ

Today we're reading about the council in Jerusalem. At the end of the council meeting, they sent a letter to the Gentile (non-Jewish) Christians. But first they had an important decision to make: Should Gentile Christians keep the Jewish law?

Read what Peter said in **Acts 15v11** (*With older children read all of Acts 15v5-11*)

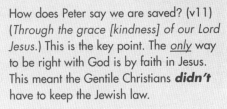

TALK

How does Peter say we are saved? (v11) (*Through the grace [kindness] of our Lord Jesus.*) This is the key point. The _only_ way to be right with God is by faith in Jesus. This meant the Gentile Christians **didn't** have to keep the Jewish law.

DO

Copy v11 onto some paper: "We believe it is through the grace of our Lord Jesus that we are saved." Stick it on the wall.

The council sent a letter back with Paul. **Read v30-31** to see what the letter did. (*It encouraged the new Christians.*)

PRAY

Can you send a letter or email to a (new?) Christian you know? Encourage them to keep following Jesus. Add v11 to your letter. **Pray for them now.**

Building up
Read Acts 15v19-21 What did James say they shouldn't do? (*Make it hard for the Gentiles.*) But James didn't want to make things hard for the Jewish believers either. So he told the Gentiles to avoid doing things that would offend the Jewish Christians (v20-21). Ask God to help you tell your friends about Jesus, and not to do anything that might put them off turning to Him.

DAY 3
What a barny

KEYPOINT
Paul and Barnabas argued and split up—but God brought good out of it.

Today's passages are:
Table Talk: Acts 15v36-41
XTB: Acts 15v36-41

TABLE TALK

Do you ever have arguments? What about? How do you feel afterwards?

READ

It was time for Paul to set off on his 2nd Missionary Journey. His mission was to see how the new Christians were getting on, and to tell more people about Jesus. Paul wanted Barnabas to join him, but they had an argument about who else to take. **Read Acts 15v36-41**

TALK

Who did Barnabas want to take? (v37) (*John Mark—Barnabas' cousin.*) Why didn't Paul's want to take him? (v38) (*J-M had travelled with them before, but had given up part way.*) Paul and Barnabas had a big argument about it, and decided to split up. Where did Barnabas and J-M go? (v39) (*Cyprus*) Where did Paul and Silas go? (v41) (*Through Syria and Cilicia.*)

THINK

This is a sad story, but look how God used it for good. Instead of _one_ journey, now there were _two_ journeys, and _two_ places that would hear about Jesus. God took this **sad** event and brought **good** out of it! Thank God that He can do this.

PRAY

Ask God to help you not to spoil your friendships with arguments. Ask Him to help you to say sorry and put things right if you do.

Building up
John Mark was sometimes called John and sometimes Mark! He's the same guy who wrote Mark's Gospel. Paul's view of John Mark seems to have changed later. Check out **Colossians 4v10** and **2 Timothy 4v11**

DAY 4
A puzzling choice

KEYPOINT
Paul circumcised Timothy, to make it easier for other Jews to accept him and listen to him.

Today's passages are:
Table Talk: Acts 16v1-3
XTB: Acts 16v1-5

TABLE TALK

How many names can you think of beginning with **T**?

READ

When Paul and Silas reached the town of Lystra, they met **Timothy**. Paul wanted to take Timothy with them, but he decided to do something very puzzling first.
Read Acts 16v1-3

DO

Use verse 1 to fill in the **Family Tree**.

TALK

Jewish boys were circumcised (a small piece of skin cut off) when they were 8 days old. But although Timothy's mum was Jewish, his dad wasn't, so Timothy hadn't been circumcised. What did Paul do? (v3) (*Circumcised Timothy.*) Why? (v3) (*Because the Jews knew that Tim's dad was a Greek, and therefore Timothy hadn't been circumcised.*) See Notes for Parents for more on <u>why</u> Paul did this.

PRAY

Paul was ready to do everything he could to make it easier for people to find out about Jesus. Are <u>you</u>? It can be scary talking about Jesus, and might mean making changes. (E.g. Inviting neighbours to join you at church and come for lunch afterwards—even if you'd rather be on your own or crash out in front of the TV.) Ask God to help you do everything you can to tell others about Jesus.

Building up
Read Acts 16v4-5 They were telling people the decision made by the Jerusalem Council. What was the result? (v5) (*Christians were strengthened, and the churches grew.*) When God's words are taught and obeyed, Christians grow to know Him better. Ask God to help you know Him better, and to obey Him, as you read Acts together.

DAYS 4-5
Notes for Parents

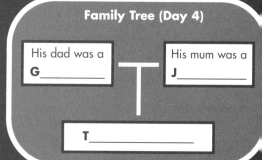

Family Tree (Day 4)

His dad was a
G_____

His mum was a
J_____

T_____

Why did Paul circumcise Timothy?

On Day 1 we saw that some people thought you had to be circumcised to be a Christian. Paul knew that was wrong. He <u>didn't</u> circumcise Timothy to make him a Christian. Timothy was <u>already</u> a Christian.

But the Jews in the area knew that Timothy wasn't circumcised. This might make it hard for them to accept him. (Jews would only accept religious teaching from other Jews.) It would also mean Timothy couldn't join Paul inside Jewish synagogues. So Paul circumcised Timothy to make it easier for other Jews to accept him and listen to what he told them about Jesus.

MAKING DECISIONS (Day 5)

Acts 16 tells us that the Holy Spirit <u>stopped</u> Paul from going to Asia or Bithynia—although it doesn't tell us how the Spirit did this. Later, we see that God showed Paul what to do in a <u>vision</u>.

We sometimes read about things like this in the Bible, but they are <u>unusual</u> ways for God to show us what to do. Usually God guides us through the **Bible**. If **you** have a decision to make, these questions will help:

1 **Is it godly?** (i.e. Does it fit with what the Bible tells us about how God wants us to live?)

2 **Is it wise?** (If you're not sure, ask an older Christian what they think.)

Pray about your decision, and ask God to help you be godly and wise.

DAY 5 Paul & Co. Where to go?

KEYPOINT
God showed Paul and Co. exactly where to go next on their missionary journey.

Today's passages are:
Table Talk: Acts 16v9-10
XTB: Acts 16v6-10

TABLE TALK

Make a simple obstacle course using chairs, cushions etc. Blindfold your child, then give them step-by-step instructions to move safely round the course.

THINK

Paul and Co. were continuing on their journey. How do you think they decided where to go? (*Get suggestions.*)

READ

Paul planned to go to Asia and Bithynia, but both times the Holy Spirit stopped him! Then Paul had a vision—a dream sent by God. **Read Acts 16v9-10**

TALK

Who did Paul see in his dream? (v9) (*A man from Macedonia, which is Northern Greece.*) What did the man say? (v9) (*Come to Macedonia and help us.*) What did Paul do? (v10) (*Got ready to go*)

THINK

On his first journey, Paul hadn't gone as far as Greece, but this time God wanted him to go further. This was the first time that the good news about Jesus reached **Europe**. Do _you_ live in Europe? Wherever you live, thank God that the great news about Jesus has reached you too.

PRAY

Ask God to help you to be as ready to obey Him as Paul was.

Building up
Read about **Making Decisions** in **Notes for Parents** on the previous page. Which do you think is hardest?—Knowing what God wants you to do, or being ready to obey Him no matter what He says? Pray together about your answers.

DAY 6 Purple page

KEYPOINT
Lydia became a believer, then offered her home to Paul and the others to stay in.

Today's passages are:
Table Talk: Acts 16v13-15
XTB: Acts 16v11-15

TABLE TALK

Give everyone one minute to collect something **purple**.

Purple used to be a very expensive colour to make. So purple cloth was mainly worn by rich or important people. (That's why we think of it as a royal colour.)

READ

When Paul and Co. reached Macedonia, they went to the city of **Philippi**. There they met a woman who sold purple cloth. **Read Acts 16v13-15**

TALK

Why did Paul and the others go to the river? (v13) (*They were looking for a place of prayer.*) Who did they meet there? (v13,14) (*Some women, including Lydia, a dealer in purple cloth.*) When Lydia heard the great news about Jesus she became a Christian. What did she do next? (v15) (*She was baptised, then invited Paul & Co. to stay at her home, which probably became the meeting place for the Christians in Philippi.*)

PRAY

Lydia wanted to **help** Paul. Do _you_ know anyone who tells others about Jesus? How can you **help** them? (*Write to them [in purple?] to say you're praying for them? Send a present to encourage them?*) Agree what you will do, then pray for that person.

Building up
Look up **Philippi** in a Bible atlas, or **Greece** in a modern atlas. Pray for Christians living in Greece today. Ask God to help them to tell others about Jesus.

DAY 7
Go to jail

KEYPOINT
Paul freed a slave-girl from an evil spirit, but ended up in jail as a result.

Today's passages are:
Table Talk: Acts 16v16-18 & 23-24
XTB: Acts 16v16-24

TABLE TALK

A few years ago, at a school fair, I was put into the stocks. The children lined up to throw wet sponges at me! Can you guess why? (*To raise money.*) In today's story, Paul and Silas end up in the stocks too...

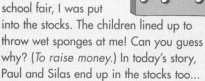

READ

In Philippi, Paul and Silas met a slave girl. She was being controlled by an evil spirit. This meant that she could tell the future. Her owners made a lot of money from her fortune telling.
Read Acts 16v16-18

TALK

Paul told the evil spirit to leave the girl. In whose name was Paul speaking? (v18) (*The name of **Jesus**.*) Did the spirit leave her? (v18) (*Yes!*)

READ

The owners of the slave girl were furious! They told lies about Paul and Silas to get them thrown into jail.
Read v23-24 to see where the jailer put them. (*In an inner cell, with their feet in the stocks.*)

PRAY

Sometimes people won't like it when we do the right thing (because it stops them doing something wrong). Ask God to help you to do what's right, even if other people make it hard for you.

Building up
This slave girl knew that Paul was a servant of the Most High God (v17), but she was involved in **evil** stuff, and Paul didn't want people to connect **Jesus** with those things. So Paul told the evil spirit it had to leave her. Why do you think the spirit obeyed? (*Paul was able to free her through **Jesus' power**. Jesus is the Most High God —and nobody is more powerful than Him!*) Thank Jesus that nobody and nothing is more powerful than Him.

DAY 8
Get out of jail free

KEYPOINT
God used Paul and Silas in jail to tell the jailer and his family all about Jesus.

Today's passages are:
Table Talk: Acts 16v25-31 & 34
XTB: Acts 16v25-34

TABLE TALK

Recap yesterday's story: Paul and Silas had been beaten, thrown into jail and chained up. How do you think they <u>felt</u>?

READ

Read Acts 16v25

What were Paul and Silas doing? (*Praying and singing!*)

What a shock! But it wasn't the only shoc that night... **Read Acts 16v26-31**

What happened at midnight? (v26) (*An earthquake—the doors opened and the chains fell off.*)

DO

Act out an earthquake in your room!

TALK

What did the jailer think had happened? (v27) (*They had escaped.*) The jailer knew he would be blamed, and probably killed for it, so he drew his sword to kill himself. Who stopped him? (v28) (*Paul*) The jailer was amazed they hadn't tried t escape. He asked Paul how he could be saved. What did Paul say? (v31) (*Believe in Jesus.*) When Paul told the jailer and his family about Jesus, they all believed. They were baptised as Christians.

PRAY

Read v34 The jailer was full of **joy** because he was now a follower of Jesus. Are <u>you</u> following Jesus? Does that fill yo with <u>joy</u>? Pray about your answers.

Building up
Look back to the jailer's question in **v30**. How would <u>you</u> answer his question? Read the rest of the story in **v35-40**. What did Paul do before he left Philippi? (v40) (*Went to Lydia's house to encourage the Christians meeting there.*) Later Paul also wrote to them. Read the start of his letter in **Philippians 1v1-6**

DAY 9
The King has come

KEYPOINT
Jesus is the Christ/Messiah, God's Chosen King.

Today's passages are:
Table Talk: Acts 17v1-4
XTB: Acts 17v1-10

BLE LK

How many names can you think of for the ruler of a country? (*Queen, President, Emperor...*)

EAD

Christ (in Greek) and **Messiah** (in Hebrew) both mean "God's Chosen King". In today's verses Paul is teaching about this King. **Read Acts 17v1-4**

ALK

Paul and Silas had travelled 100 miles from Philippi. Where were they now? (v1) (*Thessalonica*) Paul went to the synagogue, and taught the people from the Old Testament (the Scriptures). What did he say the Christ (Messiah) had to do? (v3) (*Suffer and rise from the dead*)

INK

<u>Why</u> did Jesus have to suffer and rise from the dead? (*He died to take the punishment for our sins. God brought Him back to life to show that He accepted Jesus' death in our place.*) We'll look at this in more detail on Day 13

Some people <u>believed</u> what Paul was teaching about Jesus, and became Christians. But others were <u>jealous</u>, and started a riot. (*This is in verses 5-9*). Paul and Silas had to escape to Berea.

AY

Thank God for sending Jesus as our King, just as He promised to do.

Building up
Look back at what Paul taught on his <u>first</u> missionary journey—spot how he used the Old T to show that Jesus had to suffer and rise from the dead. **Read Acts 13v26-38** Now look up another Old T passage about Jesus' death for our sins. **Read Isaiah 53v4-6** Thank God for keeping His promise to send Jesus as our Saviour King.

DAY 10
Check it out!

KEYPOINT
The Bereans checked that what Paul said really did come from the Bible.

Today's passages are:
Table Talk: Acts 17v10-12
XTB: Acts 17v10-15

TABLE TALK

Think of some words starting with **Check** (*Checkout, Check-Up, Checkmate...*) What does each one mean?

READ

Check out where Paul and Silas went next. **Read Acts 17v10-12**

What city were they in? (v10) (*Berea*) Did the Bereans listen to Paul's message? (v11) (*Yes!*) They also checked Paul out! What did they check with? (v11) (*The Scriptures, the Old T part of the Bible.*) Having checked carefully, did they believe what Paul said? (v12) (*Yes—many Jews and Greeks believed.*)

TALK

THINK

Why do you think the Bereans <u>checked</u> what Paul was saying?

PRAY

The Bible tells us everything we need to know about Jesus. Thank God for giving us the Bible. Ask Him to help you to understand it as you read it.

Dear Table Talk readers,
When I write Table Talk and XTB I do my very best to get it right. But I'm not perfect! Sometimes I might make a mistake. So please read the Bible for yourselves, just like the Bereans, and check that what I've written really is true! Thank you.
Alison

Building up
Read the rest of the story in **Acts 17v13-15** Yet again Paul's enemies made trouble for him, and he had to leave. Where did he go next? (v15) (*Athens*) Did this leave the Bereans with no-one to teach them? (*No—Silas and Timothy stayed there for a while.*)

DAY 11
Idol talk

Today's passages are:
Table Talk: Acts 17v16-18
XTB: Acts 17v16-18

TABLE TALK

Athens is the capital of Greece. It is full of ancient buildings and beautiful statues. Find Athens in an atlas or encyclopaedia.

READ

Paul left Berea and went to Athens. As you read the verses, listen for the answer to 4 questions: What did Paul See? Feel? Do? and Say? **Read Acts 17v16-18**

TALK

What did Paul see? (v16) (A city full of idols—statues of pretend gods.)

What did Paul feel? (v16) (Distressed and upset.)

What did Paul do? (v17) (He went to the synagogue and market-place to talk with those who were there.)

What did Paul say? (v18) (He told them the good news about Jesus, who had risen from the dead.)

Note: The Epicureans and Stoics were from two schools of philosophy. They held different religious beliefs.

PRAY

Like the people in Athens, most people today know very little about Jesus. Think of **four things** you could tell someone about Jesus. Ask God to help you to tell someone about Jesus this week.

Building up
Many people today are more interested in money, sport, pop music or clothes than in Jesus. These are their "idols". Think of some popular TV programmes that show this to be true. Pray for any friends who think these things are more important than Jesus. Ask God to help you to tell them about Jesus.

DAY 12
What's God like?

Today's passages are:
Table Talk: Acts 17v22-25
XTB: Acts 17v19-28

TABLE TALK

Tell each other some **Knock, Knock** jc

Paul was taken to speak at the city council in Athens, the **Areopagus**.

That's a cue for one more joke:
Knock, Knock. Who's there? 'Arr
'Arry who? Areopagus!

READ

While walking round Athens, Paul hac seen many altars, where people gave gifts to their gods. He spoke about one those altars to the people at the Areopagus. **Read Acts 17v22-25**

TALK

What was written on one of the altars? (v23) (To an unknown god.) Paul told people all about this God they didn't know. What did he tell them? (v24-25 (God _made_ the world and everything it, including all the people. He _rules_ t world—He is Lord of heaven and ear

THINK

God is completely different from idols. The idols in Athens were just statues made by human hands. **But God isn** God _made_ and _rules_ everything!

PRAY

Paul needed to tell the people in Athen about God because they didn't know Him. Thank God that **we** can get to know Him by reading His word to us, Bible. Ask Him to help you to know Hi better and better as you read the Bible

Building up
Read the next part of Paul's speech in **Acts 17v26-28** What else does Paul teach the Athenians about God? (See v26 & v27) Writ **"What's God like?"** at the top of a sheet o paper. Use Paul's speech in v24-28 to list som answers. Thank God for being like this.

Jesus the Judge

KEYPOINT
Paul told his listeners that Jesus will be their Judge.

Today's passages are:
Table Talk: Acts 17v29-31
XTB: Acts 17v29-34

TABLE TALK

Recap what Paul told the Athenians about God. (*He made us and rules us.*)

READ

Since God made us all, we are all <u>His</u> children (His offspring). Paul then told the Athenians what that meant they had to <u>do</u>. **Read Acts 17v29-31**

TALK

What did Paul tell the people they had to do? (v30) (*To repent, to turn from their wrong ways.*) Why? (v31) (*A day is coming when we will all be judged by Jesus.*) How could they be sure about this? (v31) (*Because God raised Jesus from the dead.*)

Use **Notes for Parents** opposite to see how Jesus is our *Judge*, and also our *Rescuer*.

PRAY

Thank God for sending Jesus to rescue you.

WANT TO KNOW MORE?
For a free booklet called **Why did Jesus die?** write to us at Table Talk, 37 Elm Road, New Malden, Surrey, KT3 3HB

Or email us at: Alison@thegoodbook.co.uk

Building up
Paul took every opportunity to tell people about Jesus. This speech was based on the altar to "an unknown god" that he spotted while walking round Athens. Read how people reacted in **Acts 17v32-34** If someone asked <u>you</u> why you are a follower of Jesus what would you say? Ask God to help you take every opportunity to talk about Jesus.

Notes for Parents

JESUS IS OUR JUDGE AND RESCUER
(You need pencil and paper.) *Draw a person (a stick man is fine) on the paper.*

Paul told the people in Athens that a day is coming when we will <u>all</u> be judged by Jesus. But there's a problem! We are all <u>guilty</u>—because we all <u>sin</u>.

ASK: What is sin?
Sin is more than just doing wrong things. We all like to be **in charge** of our own lives. We do what **we** want instead of what **God** wants. This is called Sin.

Because we all sin, we are all guilty.

Write GUILTY on your picture.

GUILTY

ASK: What does sin do?
Sin gets in the way between us and God. It stops us from knowing God and from being His friends.

But the great news is that Jesus came to rescue us from our sins! If we believe in Jesus, we will still be judged, but we will be found Not Guilty!

Add NOT to your picture.

NOT GUILTY

ASK: Why will we be found "Not Guilty"?
When Jesus died on the cross He was being punished. He took the punishment that we deserve, so that we can be forgiven. He was found Guilty, so that we can be found Not Guilty.

If we believe in Jesus there is nothing to get in the way between us and God any more. Nothing to stop us knowing Him and being His friends. Jesus has <u>rescued</u> us from our sin.

DAY 14
Intent on teaching

KEYPOINT
Paul worked as a tentmaker so that he wouldn't be a burden on the Christians in Corinth.

Today's passages are:
Table Talk: Acts 18v1-5
XTB: Acts 18v1-5

 TABLE TALK
If you can, put up a play tent or make a simple tent by draping a sheet over a table. Sit inside the tent to do Table Talk.

 READ
When Paul left Athens he went to Corinth. **Read Acts 18v1-5**

 TALK
We're coming to the end of Paul's 2nd Missionary Journey. What has his mission always been? (*Telling people about Jesus.*) But now he's doing another job as well. What? (v3) (*Making tents.*)

 THINK
Paul could have asked the Christians in Corinth for money. Why do you think he didn't? (*Get suggestions.*) Paul told them why in a letter he wrote later. He said he didn't want to be a burden to them. (*If you have time, read 2 Corinthians 11v9.*)

Who joined Paul in Corinth? (v5) (*Silas and Timothy.*) They brought gifts and money with them. What could Paul do now? (*Use all his time for teaching.*)

 PRAY
Pray for someone you know who teaches about Jesus. Ask God to give them all they need to keep teaching about Jesus.

Building up
In Corinth, Paul met Priscilla and Aquila. Find out more about them in **Acts 18v18-28** and **Romans 16v3-4**. God used this team of husband and wife to teach people about Jesus. Do you know a married couple who teach others about Jesus? Pray for them, and ask God to help them.

DAY 15
Journey's end

KEYPOINT
Peter tells his listeners that Jesus is both their Judge and their Rescue

Today's passages are:
Table Talk: Acts 10v42-43
XTB: Acts 10v42-43

 TABLE TALK
Write "Don't be afraid" in a speech bubble. When might someone say that to you? (*E.g. In a thunderstorm, before an exam, when you see a spider...*) Today someone says this to Paul.

Don't be afraid!

 READ
It's the end of Paul's 2nd Missionary Journey. He's in Corinth, teaching Jewish people about Jesus. But some of the Jews became angry and tried to stop him, so he started teaching the Gentiles (non-Jews) instead. Then one night Paul had a dream. **Read Acts 18v9-11**

 TALK
Who did Paul see in his dream? (v11) (*JESUS. Luke, who wrote Acts, often used "the Lord" to mean Jesus.*) What did Jesus say? (*See v11 & 12.*) Jesus promised that no-one in Corinth would harm Paul. So Paul stayed for a long time. How long? (v11) (*A year & a half*)

PRAY
All through Paul's journey he kept on telling people about Jesus. Even when things got tough, or people tried to stop him, he carried on speaking. Do you find it hard to tell people about Jesus? Ask God to help you to be like Paul, and to keep on speaking even when it's hard.

Building up
Paul's mission was to tell people about Jesus. Most of us won't ever be travelling missionaries like he was, so what should we be doing? Look up Paul's answer in his letter to the Colossians. **Read Colossians 3v17** Ask God to help you to honour Jesus in all that you do.

DAY 16-25
Notes for Parents

THE BACKGROUND TO EXODUS

At the beginning of the book of Exodus, the Israelites are living in Ancient Egypt.

If your children know the story of Joseph, ask them to tell you the main points: Jacob and his family were living in Canaan (the land God had promised). Joseph's brothers hated him, and sold him to be a slave in Egypt. God used Joseph to rescue his family from a terrible famine in Canaan. They went to Egypt, where there was plenty to eat.

The family settled down in Egypt, and lived there for the next 400 years. That's where Exodus picks the story up.

THE ISRAELITES

The Israelites were all the family of one man—Abraham. God had made three amazing promises to Abraham:

1 **LAND** (God promised to give Abraham's family the land of Canaan to live in.)

2 **CHILDREN** (God said that Abraham's family would be so HUGE that there would be too many to count.)

3 **BLESSING** (God promised that someone from Abraham's family would be God's way of blessing the whole world.)

DAY 16
Oodles of Israelites

KEYPOINT
It's 400 years since the time of Joseph. The Israelites are still in Egypt, but as slaves.

Today's passages are:
Table Talk: Exodus 1v8-11
XTB: Exodus 1v1-11

TABLE TALK

Look up chapter 1 of **Exodus**. What's on the previous page? (*The end of Genesis, and the account of Joseph.*) Use **Notes for Parents** opposite to recap the story of Joseph.

READ

Exodus picks up the story of the Israelites 400 years later. By then there were oodles of them! **Read Exodus 1v8-11**

TALK

What did the new king (Pharaoh) <u>not</u> know? (v8) (*About Joseph, who saved the <u>Egyptians</u> from the famine as well as the <u>Israelites</u>.*) There were so many Israelites that Pharaoh was worried. What did he think they would do? (v10) (*Help Egypt's enemies.*) So what did Pharaoh do? (*Make the Israelites into slaves.*)

THINK

Read about the God's three promises to Abraham in **Notes for Parents**. <u>Pharaoh</u> wanted to keep the Israelites as slaves in Egypt. But what had <u>God</u> promised them? (*That they would live in Canaan.*) So the scene is set for a big showdown between God and Pharaoh. Who do you think will win? And why?

PRAY

Exodus show us very clearly what God is like. Ask God to help you to get to know Him better as you read Exodus together.

Building up
Read Exodus 1v1-7 What clues are there that God is keeping His second promise to Abraham? God <u>never</u> forgets His promises. As you read Exodus, look out for other clues that God is going to keep **all** of His promises.

DAY 17
Happy birth day?

KEYPOINT
Pharaoh told the midwives to kill the baby boys, but they feared God, not Pharaoh.

Today's passages are:
Table Talk: Exodus 1v15-17
XTB: Exodus 1v11-17

TABLE TALK

If you're a parent, how did you feel when you found out you were having a child? What did you need to get ready?

READ

Most parents are excited about having a child. But for the Israelites, having a baby became a frightening time. They were having so many children, that Pharaoh came up with a terrible plan.
Read Exodus 1v15-17

TALK

The midwives helped the Israelite women to give birth. What did Pharaoh tell the midwives to do if a boy was born? (v16) (*Kill him.*) What were they to do with a girl? (v16) (*Let her live.*) Did the midwives do what Pharaoh commanded? (v17) (*No!*) Why not? (v17) (*They feared God.*)

THINK

To *fear God* means to honour, respect and obey Him. Why do you think the midwives obeyed God rather than Pharaoh? (*Think about what you know about God and about Pharaoh.*)

PRAY

God prevented Pharaoh's evil plans, and kept the Israelite boys safe. Thank God that nothing and no-one can stop His plans from working out.

Building up
Read what happened to the midwives in **Exodus 1v18-21** Again we are told that the midwives feared God (v21). What did God give them? (*Families of their own.*) And what happened to the Israelites? (v20) (*Their numbers continued to grow.*) God was still keeping His second promise to Abraham! (*See yesterday's Notes for Parents.*)

DAY 18
Saved!

KEYPOINT
God used Pharaoh's own daughter to stop Pharaoh's evil plan. God is the real King.

Today's passages are:
Table Talk: Exodus 2v7-10
XTB: Exodus 1v22-2v10

TABLE TALK

Note: *Read Ex 2v1-10 beforehand so you can tell it in your own words.*

Play **Hangman** to guess the question: "Who is the King?"

This important question runs through the book of Exodus. Pharaoh was king of Egypt. He thought he was the most important king there was. But who did the midwives obey yesterday? (*God*)

READ

Pharaoh made another horrible decision. He said that all Israelite boys must be drowned in the river Nile. But today's story shows very clearly that **God** is the real King (not Pharaoh!).

With older children: read all of **v1-10**.
With younger children: retell the story of baby Moses to the point where his sister brings his mum to see Pharaoh's daughter. **Read Exodus 2v7-10**

TALK

Who found Moses in the river? (*Pharaoh's daughter.*) Who brought Moses up? (*Pharaoh's daughter!*)

PRAY

Wow! God used Pharaoh's own daughter to stop Pharaoh's evil plan! Thank God that He's always in control.

Building up
Check back to **Notes for Parents** on Day 16 to see what's God's third promise was. (*Blessing.*) **Read Exodus 1v22** Pharaoh tried to use the Nile to destroy the Israelites. (*If all the boys were killed they would eventually die out, and God's plan for someone from this family to bless the whole world would fail.*) Instead, God used the river to save the Israelites (by saving Moses). **Praise God** for being so wonderful!

DAY 19
Who chose you?

KEYPOINT
Moses tried to help the Israelites, then fled from Egypt when they rejected his rule over them.

Today's passages are:
Table Talk: Exodus 2v11-15
XTB: Exodus 2v11-15

BLE LK

Imagine what it was like for Moses to grow up in Pharaoh's palace. What may he have learnt? (*E.g. to speak Egyptian, drive a chariot, read hieroglyphics...*)

EAD

Moses would have dressed like an Egyptian (the men wore make-up and wigs!). But he <u>wasn't</u> an Egyptian, he was an *Israelite* (a Hebrew).
Read Exodus 2v11-15

LK

Moses was now 40 years old. One day, he saw an Egyptian beating an Israelite slave. What did Moses do? (v12) (*Killed the Egyptian and hid him.*) The next day, Moses saw two Israelites fighting. When he tried to stop them, what did they say? (v14) (*"Who made you our ruler and judge? Will you kill us too?"*) When Moses realised they knew what he had done, he was scared. Later, Pharaoh found out, so Moses had to escape. Where did he go? (v15) (*Midian*)

INK

It wasn't <u>yet</u> the right time for Moses to lead the Israelites—they hadn't even asked God for help yet!—but God had <u>already</u> chosen Moses as their rescuer. When it was the **right time**, God would bring Moses back to Egypt.

AY

Matthew 6v8 says, "Your Father already knows what you need before you ask Him." Thank God that He knows <u>your</u> needs before you ask Him about them.

Building up
Check out what the book of Acts tells us about this story. **Read Acts 7v23-29** What did Moses think the Israelites would know? (v25) (*That God was using him to rescue them.*) But they didn't. The time wasn't yet right.

DAY 20
Crying out to God

KEYPOINT
Moses spent 40 years in Midian. Then the Israelites cried to God for help.

Today's passages are:
Table Talk: Exodus 2v15-25
XTB: Exodus 2v15-25

DO

On small bits of paper draw a stick man for Moses, one for Jethro (Reuel), a group of seven for Jethro's daughters, and some sheep. Use these as you tell the story.

READ

Moses was 40 when he ran away to Midian, where he lived for 40 years. Read **Exodus 2v15-22** aloud, as your child moves the pictures to show what's happening.

Meanwhile, back in Egypt the king died. There was now a new king—also called Pharaoh! **Read Exodus 2v23-25**

The Israelites were still slaves. What did they do? (v23) (*Cried to God for help.*)

THINK

At last the Israelites had turned to God for help. But God started answering their prayer long ago! Moses was **40** when he went to Midian, and he lived there for **40** years. So how old was he now? (*80*) That means God started to answer the Israelites' prayer 80 years before they even asked Him!!

PRAY

We don't know what <u>our</u> needs will be in a year's time—but God does! He <u>always</u> knows what we need and what will be best for us. How does that make you feel? Talk to God about your answers.

Building up
Read v24-25 again. Verse 24 says "God *remembered* His covenant." God doesn't <u>forget</u>! This means that He **acted** on His promises. Look up another time when God "remembered" a promise in **Genesis 8v1**. God always keeps His promises, at the time that He knows to be right. Praise Him for being like this.

THE BURNING BUSH (Day 21)

At last it was the right time for God to send Moses back to Egypt...

Moses was looking after the sheep...

...when he saw a bush that was on fire.

But the fire wasn't burning the bush!

When Moses went closer, he heard a voice.
MOSES! MOSES!

Here I am.

I am the God of your father, the God of Abraham, Isaac and Jacob.

Taken from Exodus 3v1-6

BIBLE NAMES (Day 22)

Bible names aren't just names. They also tell you something about the person. The name Moses means "pull out". Do you remember who pulled Moses out of the river when he was a baby? (Check in Exodus 2v10)

KEYPOINT
God speaks to Moses from a non-burning bush. It's time for Moses to go to Egypt.

Today's passages are:
Table Talk: Exodus 3v7-10
XTB: Exodus 3v1-10

TABLE TALK

Recap: How old was Moses when he ran away from Egypt? (*40*) How long d he stay in Midian? (*40 years*) So how old is he now? (*80*) Read the picture story in **Notes for Parents** opposite see what happened next.

READ

Read the Bible verses to find out what else God said to Moses.
Read Exodus 3v7-10

TALK

What did God say He was going to do? (v8) (*Rescue the Israelites, and bring them to the land of Canaan.*) Which of God's promises to Abraham is He keeping? (*See Notes for Parents on Da 16 for summary of God's three promise to Abraham.*) The time had now come f God to keep His promise about the **lan** Who was God going to send to rescue His people? (v10) (*Moses*)

PRAY

Thank God that He always keeps His promises.

Building up

Read the full story in **Exodus 3v1-6** Why was Moses to take off his sandals? (*Because the ground was holy.*) Holy means "set apart".
God is holy. There is no-one like Him. He alone is perfect and morally pure.
Read 1 Samuel 2v2
Spend some time praising our holy God.

DAY 22
What's in a name?

KEYPOINT
God gave Moses His name:
I AM WHO I AM.

Today's passages are:
Table Talk: Exodus 3v10-15
XTB: Exodus 3v10-15

TABLE TALK

Talk about your names, and why they were chosen. Do you know what your names mean? (*John means "gift of God", Sarah means "princess" and Alison [my name!] means "noble".*)

Read about **Bible names** in **Notes for Parents** opposite.

READ

God is still speaking from the burning bush. He tells Moses His name.
Read Exodus 3v10-15

TALK

Moses knows he can't rescue the Israelites by himself. But what does God promise him? (v12) (*To be with Moses.*) What name did God give Himself? (v14) (*I AM WHO I AM.*)

THINK

What do you think this name tells us about God? (*God never changes. He is everlasting. He is always with us.*)

PRAY

Think for a while about **God**, the great **I AM**. Then thank and praise Him for being like this.

Building up
Look up Matthew 1v21 to see why **Jesus** was given His name. The name Jesus means "God saves." Why is this a great name for Jesus? (*It tells us who Jesus is—He is God. And it tells us what Jesus does—He saves us.*)

DAY 23
Planning to go

KEYPOINT
God told Moses His <u>plans</u>, and also what the <u>results</u> would be.

Today's passages are:
Table Talk: Exodus 3v18-20
XTB: Exodus 3v16-20

TABLE TALK

Make a plan to do something together this week. (*Swimming, go out for an ice-cream, weed the garden!*) Write your plan on some paper and stick it on the wall where you can all see it.

READ

God—the great "I AM"—is still talking to Moses from the burning bush. He tells Moses about His <u>plans</u> to rescue the Israelites. Moses is to go to the leaders (elders) of the Israelites, and tell them God's plans. **Read Exodus 3v18-20**

TALK

God didn't just tell Moses His <u>plans</u>. He also told Him the <u>results</u>! Will the Israelite leaders listen to Moses? (v18) (*Yes*) Will Pharaoh let them go as God commands? (v19) (*No*) So God will send terrifying plagues to strike Egypt. What will Pharaoh do then? (v20) (*Let them go.*)

PRAY

God is the great "I AM". He knew everything that would happen to the Israelites. He knows everything that will happen to <u>you</u> too! He knows about the plans you've made, about your family, your school, work... Thank God that He knows everything about you. Ask Him to help you to trust Him with every part of your life.

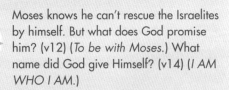

Building up
The Israelites had been poor slaves for years. But God planned it so that they wouldn't be poor when they left Egypt. **Read Exodus 3v21-22** The Israelites wouldn't just escape with their lives. They would also take the wealth of Egypt with them! **Thank God** that He generously gives us all we need, and much more as well.

DAY 24
Snake sign

KEYPOINT
God gave Moses three signs to show that God had sent him.

Today's passages are:
Table Talk: Exodus 4v1-9
XTB: Exodus 4v1-9

TABLE TALK

Recap: Why did Moses run away from Egypt 40 years earlier? (*Pharaoh found out that Moses had killed an Egyptian.*) *If you have time, recap the story from Day 19*

READ

At that time, Moses had been trying to help the Israelites—but they <u>didn't believe</u> he had the right to lead them. (*Ex 2v14*) This time it's important that the Israelites know that **God** has chosen Moses to be their leader. **Read Exodus 4v1-9**

DO

Now read it again, with your child miming the three signs.

TALK

What did the staff turn into? (v3) (*A snake.*) What happened to Moses' hand? (v6) (*It had a skin disease, covering it in white spots.*) What happened to the water? (v9) (*It turned to blood.*)

PRAY

These three signs showed the Israelites that Moses really had been sent by God. **Psalm 19v1** says that the sky is like a <u>sign</u> for us, showing us how great God is. What does the sky look like now? What was it like yesterday? Thank God that the sky reminds us He is our great Creator.

Building up

These signs were amazing, but there's a far more astounding sign in the New Testament. **Read Acts 17v31** (*We looked at this verse on Day 13.*) Paul is saying that the resurrection is a <u>sign</u>. It shows that Jesus will be our **Judge**. But it also points to Jesus as our **Rescuer**. Read what Paul wrote in **Romans 4v25** When God brought Jesus back to life it showed that He accepted Jesus' death for us as the way to be forgiven. **Thank God** for Jesus, who died and rose again as our Rescuer.

DAY 25
Excuse me

KEYPOINT
God was angry when Moses wasn't willing to obey Him. But He was also patient.

Today's passages are:
Table Talk: Exodus 4v10-15
XTB: Exodus 4v10-17

TABLE TALK

Make up some funny excuses together. E.g. I don't have my homework because a camel ate it; I can't tidy my bedroom because there's a dragon guarding the door; I can't wash the dishes because...

READ

God has given Moses <u>three signs</u> to show the Israelites, but Moses is still making excuses. **Read Exodus 4v10-12**

TALK

What is Moses' excuse? (v10) (*He's not good at making speeches.*) What does God remind Moses? (v11) (*God gives us the ability to speak, hear & see.*) What does God promise?(v12) (*To help Moses.*)

But Moses still didn't want to go. **Read Exodus 4v13-15** What did Moses say? (v13) (*Send someone else.*)

THINK

Verse 14 says God was angry with Moses. Why do you think He was angry? (*Moses wasn't willing to obey Him.*) But God was also very patient with Moses. Who did He give Moses as his helper? (v14) (*Moses' brother Aaron.*) Aaron was a good speaker. He could help Moses to obey God.

PRAY

Do you sometimes make excuses, instead of obeying God? Say sorry to God for disobeying Him. Ask Him to help you to obey Him and not make excuses.

Building up

Check out what happened next in **v18-20**. Did Moses obey God? (v20) (*Yes*) Why did he take his staff? (*See v17*) We'll return to Exodus on Day 46, when we'll see how Pharaoh reacts to Moses' return.

DAY 26-45
Notes for Parents

MATTHEW MATTERS

Matthew's book about Jesus helps us to answer two big questions:

- **Who is Jesus?**
- **Why did He come?**

As we read the next part of Matthew, we'll find some answers to these questions. We'll also meet some people who <u>did</u> work out who Jesus is, and some others who <u>didn't</u>.

MAKE A DISPLAY

Matthew's book is a bit like a jigsaw, building up a picture of who Jesus is and why He came. As you read Matthew, you will find it helpful to build a display, adding information as you find it. If possible, put the display somewhere where you can all see it as you do Table Talk together.

WHO IS JESUS?

WHY DID JESUS COME?

Write each new answer on a small sheet of paper or a sticky note. Then add it to your display. Your children may like to add pictures as well.

DAY 26
Only Jesus?

KEYPOINT
The people in Nazareth rejected Jesus. They didn't believe that He was God.

Today's passages are:
Table Talk: Matthew 13v53-58
XTB: Matthew 13v53-58

DO

Make a display as shown in **Notes for Parents**. In the next few readings Matthew gives us clues to <u>who</u> Jesus is.

READ

Jesus went to Nazareth, the town where He grew up.
Read Matthew 13v53-58

TALK

How did the people react at first? (v54) (*They were amazed by His wisdom and power.*) But these people already knew Jesus from when He was growing up. What did they know about Him? (v55-56) (*His dad's a carpenter, His mum is Mary, He has 4 brothers and some sisters.*) These people know Jesus' family, and so they decided He <u>couldn't</u> be special. What did they do? (v57) (*They rejected / took offence at Jesus.*)

DO

On some paper, draw a sad face and write **"In Nazareth they didn't believe in Jesus."**
Add it to the "Who is Jesus?" display.

PRAY

These people ignored the amazing things Jesus did and said. "Dear God, help us not to ignore the amazing things we read about Jesus. Help us to believe that He really is God. Amen"

Building up
Read v58 again.
Why didn't Jesus do many miracles in Nazareth? (*Because of their lack of faith.*) Look up **John 20v30-31** to see what Jesus' miracles did. His miracles are like signposts pointing to **who** Jesus is. But the people in Nazareth <u>ignored</u> the miracles, and <u>refused</u> to believe that Jesus was God. They'd already decided to reject Jesus—so He didn't do many miracles.

DAY 27
Dead wrong

KEYPOINT
Herod was very wrong about Jesus. He thought Jesus was John the Baptist come back to life.

Today's passages are:
Table Talk: Matthew 14v1-4
XTB: Matthew 14v1-12

TABLE TALK

Think back to the Christmas story. What's the name of the evil king who tried to have the young Jesus killed? (Look up Matthew 2v13 to check your answer.)

READ

30 years later, Herod's <u>son</u> was now the ruler (called "tetrarch") in Galilee. He was also called Herod! He had married his brother's wife. But John the Baptist kept telling him that this was against God's law, so Herod had John arrested, and later killed.
Read Matthew 14v1-4

TALK

Who did Herod think Jesus was? (v2) (*John the Baptist.*) But John was dead! So what did Herod think had happened? (v2) (*John had come back to life.*)

THINK

Arresting & killing John was <u>very wrong</u>. If Herod thought Jesus was really John come back to life, he was probably <u>very scared</u>. But these weren't Herod's biggest problems. His biggest problem was that he didn't see **who** Jesus really was.

DO

Add another note to your display:
 "Herod was very wrong about Jesus."

THINK

Herod hated it when John told him that he had disobeyed God. How do <u>you</u> react when someone in your family or at church shows you that you are disobeying God?

PRAY

Ask God to help you to be ready to listen and to change.

Building up
See **Notes for Parents** for ideas for building on this passage.

DAYS 27-28
Notes for Parents

HEROD'S ACTIONS (Day 27)

If your children are old enough, read the full account of Herod's actions in Matthew 14v3-12.

Herod broke Jewish law at least four times in this horrid story: He divorced his wife (illegal in Jewish law), remarried his half-brother's wife (illegal), made a rash promise to his step-daughter at his birthday party, and got tricked by his new wife into beheading (illegal) John without a trial (illegal). *There is a fuller account in Mark 6v14-29.*

Jesus Himself said that what happened to John was a pattern for what would happen later to Jesus. (This is in Matthew 17v10-13, which we'll look at on Day 47)

Like his father before him, Herod had no concern for keeping God's law. But God still used Herod for <u>His own</u> good purposes. **Read Acts 4v27-28**

Who was in control? (*God!*) Thank God that no-one and nothing can stop His plans.

Feeding Hungry Crowds (Day 28)

The crowd Jesus fed here were Jewish (unlike the Feeding of the 4000 later, when they were Gentiles). All Jews would know how God had rescued their ancestors, the Israelites, from Egypt. After escaping from Egypt, the Israelites spent 40 years wandering in the desert. There was no food, so **God** provided food for them.
Read Exodus 16v11-18 & v31

What meat did God provide? (v13) (*Quail—small birds.*) What was the bread? (v31) (*Manna, which tasted like honey biscuits.*) What did God say that this would show? (v11) (*That He is their God.*)

When Jesus fed the 5000, He too miraculously gave food to a huge crowd, just as God did in the desert. This miracle was a <u>signpost</u>, showing that **Jesus is God**.

DAY 28
Famous five

KEYPOINT
Jesus showed He is God by miraculously feeding a huge crowd, just as God had done.

Today's passages are:
Table Talk: Matthew 14v15-21
XTB: Matthew 14v13-21

TABLE TALK

(*You need an empty lunch box, paper and pencils*.) Each draw a picture of your favourite food and put it in the lunch box. What did you draw & why?

READ

When Jesus heard about John's death, He crossed over Lake Galilee to be alone. But a huge crowd followed Him. **Read Matthew 14v15-21**

TALK

Who did Jesus say could provide food for the crowd? (v16) (*The disciples*.) But how much food did they have? (v17) (*5 loaves and 2 fish—one boy's packed lunch [Jn 6v9]*.) What did Jesus do? (*See v19*) How many leftovers were there? (v20) (*12 basketfuls*) How many were fed? (v21) (*5000 men, plus women and children. Maybe 15,000 all together!*)

DO

(*Optional*) Act the story together.

THINK

In verse 16, Jesus told the disciples that <u>they</u> could feed the crowd. Why didn't they believe Him? (v17) The disciples needed to <u>remember</u> who Jesus was, and let that make a <u>difference</u> to their thinking. **So must we!**

PRAY

"Dear God, we're sorry for the times when we forget how powerful You are. Please help us to trust You, and to do what You say. Amen."

Building up
See **Notes for Parents** on previous page for Building Up ideas. Add another note to your display: **"In the Old Testament, God gave food to His people in the desert. Jesus showed that <u>He is God</u> by doing the same thing."**
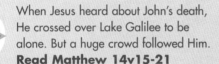

DAY 29
Sinking feeling

KEYPOINT
When Jesus walked on water, the disciples recognised that He is the Son of God.

Today's passages are:
Table Talk: Matthew 14v22-33
XTB: Matthew 14v22-33

TABLE TALK

What do you like doing at the seaside?

Today's story happened in the middle of the sea. It was just after Jesus had fed the huge crowd with five loaves and two fish. As you read the story, act it out, with someone being Peter, and someone as Jesus. **Read Matthew 14v22-33**

READ

TALK

The disciples sailed across the sea, while Jesus stayed behind, praying on a hill. How did Jesus get from the hill to the boat? (v25) (*He walked on water!*)

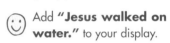
Add **"Jesus walked on water."** to your display.

Why were the disciples so scared? (v26) (*They thought He was a ghost.*) What did Peter say? (*See v28*) At first, Peter could walk on the water too. But then he started sinking. He thought the <u>wind</u> was more powerful than Jesus (v30). Was Peter right? (*No!*)

Add **"Jesus is more powerful than the wind."** to your display.

What did the disciples say at the end? (v33) (*"Truly you are the Son of God!"*) The disciples were right. But as we'll see, they still had a lot to learn.

PRAY

Read v31 again. Jesus wanted the disciples to believe that He is God and that they can <u>trust</u> Him. Ask Him to help you believe that too.

Building up
Read Matthew 14v13&23 Jesus is God's Son, but it was still important for Him to spend time alone, praying. Do you pray every day? How can you help each other to do so? Pray together now.

DAY 30
It's Jesus!

Today's passages are:
Table Talk: Matthew 14v34-36
XTB: Matthew 14v34-36

TABLE TALK

Use the map below to recap what we've read so far about Jesus.

DO

In **Nazareth** they rejected Jesus. *Draw a sad face on the map.* ☹

Jesus fed a huge crowd by the **Sea of Galilee**, then walked on the water to cross the sea! *Draw Jesus walking across the Sea of Galilee.*

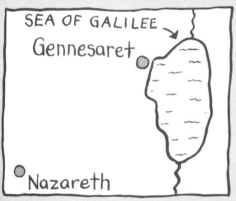

SEA OF GALILEE →

Gennesaret

Nazareth

READ

Now Jesus had reached Gennesaret.
Read Matthew 14v34-36

TALK

What did the people in Gennesaret do? (v35) (*Told everyone that Jesus was there.*) These people believed that Jesus could heal them. Were they right? (v36) ☺ (*Yes*) Draw a happy face by Gennesaret.

PRAY

At Gennesaret they believed that Jesus cared for them, and was more powerful than sickness. They were right! Thank God that Jesus is caring and powerful.

Building up
☺ Add **"In Gennesaret they believed in Jesus"** to your display.

DAY 31
Upside down

Today's passages are:
Table Talk: Matthew 15v1-3
XTB: Matthew 15v1-9

TABLE TALK

When do you wash your hands and why? E.g. Before a meal, or to make sure they're clean before drawing a special picture, or after using the toilet or...

READ

Today's reading seems to be about washing your hands. But it's not really...
Read Matthew 15v1-3

TALK

Who came to see Jesus? (v1) (*Pharisees and teachers of the Law—Jewish religious leaders.*) What were they cross about? (v2) (*Jesus' disciples didn't wash their hands before eating.*) But this wasn't about washing off germs! Why were the Pharisees cross? (v2) (*The disciples were breaking their traditions.*)

THINK

The religious leaders had made up lots of rules, known as "the tradition of the elders". They thought that if you kept them God would be pleased with you. Washing your hands in a special way was one of these rules. But there was a problem! The Pharisees were very serious about keeping their own traditions. But whose commands did they break? (v3) (*God's*) They made their **own** commands more important than **God's**! (See **Notes for Parents** if you want more detail about this.)

PRAY

Do you want to please God? Then do the things He commands. What are some of God's commands? (*If you're stuck, see Mark 12v29-31*). Ask God to help you obey **Him**, and make His commands the most important in your life.

Building up
See **Notes for Parents** for Building Up ideas.

DAY 31-32
Notes for Parents

UPSIDE DOWN THINKING (Day 31)

Jesus said that the Pharisees were breaking God's commands. Read His example of this in **Matthew 15v3-6**

This was like saying, "Sorry, Mum, no birthday present—I promised it to God instead." They had made their <u>own</u> rules more important than <u>God's</u>. That's upside down thinking!

Isaiah wrote about this kind of thing hundreds of years before. **Read v7-9**

Isaiah said that they honoured God with their <u>words</u>, but that's all! Their **hearts** were far from God. Their religion did nothing to solve the problem of the heart. *Jesus had more to say about that, as we'll see tomorrow.*

OUT OF THE HEART (Day 32)

Write or draw some of the wrong things you sometimes do e.g. lying, not sharing, being unkind...

DAY 32
Inside out

 KEYPOINT
The things that come from the <u>heart</u> are what separate us from God.

Today's passages are:
Table Talk: Matthew 15v10-11, 15-20
XTB: Matthew 15v10-20

 TABLE TALK

Think of some of the <u>wrong</u> things you do. Write them in the heart opposite.

 READ

The Pharisees worried about what they were like on the **outside**. They thought that breaking their rules (like not washing your hands in a special way) made you "unclean" (which meant separated from God). But Jesus said it's what you're like on the **inside** that matters to God. **Read Matthew 15v10-11**

 TALK

What did Jesus say makes us "unclean"? (v11) (*What comes out of us from inside.*) **Read Matthew 15v15-20**

Look at the things you wrote in the heart. What does Jesus say that things like these do? (v18) (*Make us "unclean"—they separate us from God.*)

 THINK

When our hands are dirty we can wash them, but we can't wash away things like these! Who <u>can</u> make our hearts clean? (*Jesus can. Being forgiven is like being washed clean on the inside.*)

 PRAY

Say **sorry** for the things you have done wrong today. **Thank** Jesus for dying for you so that you can be forgiven.

Building up
"May the words of my mouth and the thoughts of my heart be pleasing in your sight, O Lord, my Rock and my Redeemer."
Psalm 19v14
We <u>can't</u> please God on our own, but only with His help. Pray for each other, using the words from this Psalm to help you.

Little Sinners!

'What were you talking about at that conference daddy?' My 7-year-old was giving me the grand inquisition the morning after I returned from speaking at a day seminar for Youth and Children's workers. 'Sin!' I replied. 'Oh'

'And do you know what sin is?' I asked her, crunching onto a mouthful of cornflakes.

'Oh yes,' says she. 'It's all those nasty things that people who don't believe in God do. But not us. We believe in God, don't we?'

I'm a little PHARISEE ★

My jaw froze on the cereal as I realised the significance of what I'd just heard. It's official. We have a Pharisee in the family!

WHY IS IT SO DIFFICULT?

It's only people who have never had children who don't believe in Original Sin. You never have to teach children to be selfish, or cruel, or to lie. It all comes very naturally to them. It's part of our job as parents to 'socialise' our children: that is, to help them form the character and values that will enable them to live with other people. At its simplest level, this means that we teach them to share, and not to be greedy and to say 'Please' and 'Thank You.'

But because we place so much emphasis on these things—and get cross and punish children when they 'break the rules'—they naturally assume that this is what the Gospel is all about. They mistake the problem of sins with the Problem of Sin. We reward and affirm them when they are 'good', so they naturally assume that this is what God does with His children. We are pleased with them when they are well behaved, so they assume that God is pleased with them when they are well behaved. Almost automatically, we enter the Pharisee zone.

And this is made worse when the same message is being given to them at school (the authority figure is pleased with well-behaved children), and by their own sinful hearts (which delight in the pride of 'being good').

There is also the possibility that we can go to the other extreme. We can teach sin in a way that correctly emphasises its seriousness, but distorts the true picture of who we are. We need our children not only to understand how a holy God hates the sin which ruins our lives, but also shows how much value our loving God places upon us. So valuable, in fact, He sent His only Son to die for us. We may be unworthy, but we certainly are not worthless (see 1 Peter 1 v 18-19).

I'm a Doomed SINNER ★

If we do not teach sin, we will not teach a saviour. But we need to teach sin in such a way that it drives them to Jesus and the cross, and not to legalism, or the depths of despair.

A MATTER OF THE HEART

I may be teaching Granny to suck eggs, but it's important that we have crystal clear in our minds what sin actually is, otherwise we are bound to teach it wrongly; and as we have seen, the consequences of teaching it wrongly are very serious indeed.

Sin is not first and foremost the things we do. They are but the symptoms of the disease. And the disease is our desire to make **ourselves** the centre of life not **God**.

As the Lord Jesus said: "What comes out of a man is what makes him 'unclean.' For from within, out of men's hearts, come evil thoughts, sexual immorality, theft, murder, adultery, greed, malice, deceit, lewdness, envy, slander, arrogance and folly. All these evils come from inside and make a man 'unclean.'" (Mark 7:21-23). Sin is our basic inbuilt desire to do our own thing, rather than God's. And this is what we inherit as children of Adam (see Romans 5).

Sin is therefore a **relational** thing. It is about our relationship with God, and supremely about the way we have abandoned the relationship with God that we were created for. Any attempt to explain sin to children in a way which excludes God is therefore false.

I have often found that children best understand this by using the illustration of sickness. A disease (like chicken pox) is caused by some bugs that are inside your body—floating around in your blood. That is <u>what the disease is</u>. We recognise that someone <u>has</u> chicken pox because they have spots all over them, and feel hot. These are called <u>symptoms.</u> Sins—like telling lies and being unkind—are the symptoms of the disease we have in our hearts. The real disease, Sin, is that our hearts have rebelled against God. We want to be in charge, and we have pushed God out of His rightful place at the centre of our lives.

And because sin is a matter of the heart, it also means that simply reforming my behaviour will <u>never</u> deal with the problem. That would be just like sticking plasters over the spots. What I actually need is radical heart surgery if I am to become friends with God.

BUILDING BLOCKS

It follows therefore that there are several building blocks or ideas that we need to put in place with children if they are to have a correct understanding of what sin is.

GOD: children need to understand the character of God, if they are to understand who it is we have rebelled against.

Specifically, they need to know about:

★ **The Love of God.** He made them and loves them—and loves everyone else in the world also. And that is why He hates it when we are cruel or unfaithful to someone else: because He loves them.

★ **The Goodness of God.** He is the one who decides what right and wrong are. And what He says is **right** is also **good**— for us and for everybody.

★ **The Justice of God.** He is absolutely fair. He will not let sin go unpunished. And He will make sure that all things are put right.

★ **The Grace of God.** He has made it possible for sinners to be forgiven, by Jesus' death on the cross. He offers to cure our hearts of the Sin disease if we put our trust in what Jesus did on the cross.

OURSELVES: We also need to teach properly about who we are as created but fallen creatures. Particularly important is the understanding that God is a God who looks upon the heart. Our culture is one which emphasises and worships the outward appearance: be that the unreality of Barbie dolls, or the idolisation of action heroes.

Our children must know that what the Living God values above all things is a heart that loves and wants to serve Him: and that can only be created in us by the God of Grace. This we must teach and model carefully and prayerfully.
Tim Thornborough

> **If we do not teach sin, we will not teach a saviour. But we need to teach sin in such a way that it drives them to Jesus and the cross, and not to legalism, or the depths of despair.**

I'M A SINNER SAVED BY GRACE

DAY 33
Dog food

KEYPOINT
Jesus came for everyone, Gentiles as well as Jews.

Today's passages are:
Table Talk: Matthew 15v21-28
XTB: Matthew 15v21-28

TABLE TALK

Hide seven letters around the room. (*Scrabble tiles or pieces of paper, to spell GENTILE.*) Ask your children to find the letters and work out the word. What is a Gentile? (*A non-Jewish person.*)
NB: *Keep these letters for tomorrow.*

READ

The Jews were God's special people. Everyone else was called a Gentile. The woman in today's story was a Gentile.
Read Matthew 15v21-27

TALK

Why did this Gentile woman need help? (v22) (*Her daughter had a demon.*) Demons are evil spirits. They are God's enemies. But what did Jesus say? (v24 & 26) Jesus must go to the Jews **first**. He said that going to the Gentiles first would be like giving the children's food to dogs! The woman agreed! But what did she say that dogs get? (v27) (*Crumbs*)

READ

Read verse 28 Did Jesus heal the woman's daughter? (*Yes*) What did Jesus tell the woman? (*She had great faith.*) She believed that Jesus had come for the Gentiles too. And she was right!

DO

Add **"Jesus came for EVERYONE"** to the "Why did Jesus come?" display.

PRAY

Thank God that Jesus came for everyone, including you.

Building up
Read v22 again. "Son of David" was the Jewish name for the King who would rescue them (the Christ). This woman seems to understand who Jesus is.

Most of the people reading Table Talk will be Gentiles who've come to know Jesus. Are you? Thank God for the people who told you about Jesus.

DAY 34
Food for all

KEYPOINT
Jesus fed 4000+ Gentiles, as He had fed 5000+ Jews before. Jesus came for everyone.

Today's passages are:
Table Talk: Matthew 15v32-39
XTB: Matthew 15v29-39

TABLE TALK

Challenge One: (*Use yesterday's letters.*) How many words can you make from the letters in GENTILE? (Well done if you get over ten!)

Challenge Two: How many people can you feed from a few loaves and fish? (*Recap feeding the 5000 from Day 28.*)

READ

Yesterday we read about one Gentile woman who came to Jesus. Today, a huge crowd of Gentiles come to see Him. Many were sick, so Jesus healed them. The people were also hungry...
Read Matthew 15v32-39

TALK

What were the disciples worried about? (v33) (*Finding enough bread.*) They shouldn't have worried. Why not? (*Jesus had fed a crowd like this before.*) What did Jesus do? (*Fed the crowd from seven loaves and some fish.*) How much was left over? (v37) (*Seven basketfuls.*) How many were fed? (v38) (*4000 men, plus women and children.*)

THINK

Jesus fed this crowd of Gentiles just as He had fed a Jewish crowd. They shared in the amazing things Jesus did, and had the chance to believe in Him too.

Add **"Jesus wants EVERYONE to know about Him"** to your display.

PRAY

Jesus wants everyone to know about Him. Ask God to give you the courage to talk to people about Jesus.

Building up
Read **Matthew 15v29-31** Jesus healed many people. How did these Gentiles respond? (v31) (*They praised God.*) Why not do the same as them? Praise God for the great things He has done for you.

DAY 35
Sign language

KEYPOINT
There are enough signs to who Jesus is. We need to believe them.

Today's passages are:
Table Talk: Matthew 16v1-4
XTB: Matthew 16v1-4

TABLE TALK

Ask your child to draw a large fish. Then ask them (*or tell them*) the story of Jonah. (*Jonah tried to run away from God. He was thrown into the sea, swallowed by a fish, but returned safely to land after three days, Jonah 1v1-17.*)

READ

Today, some religious leaders called Pharisees and Sadducees ask Jesus for a sign. **Read Matthew 16v1-4**

TALK

What signs **do** they understand? (v2-3) (*Signs about weather*) What **don't** they understand? (v3) (*Signs of the times, i.e. signs about Jesus.*) What is the only sign they will get? (v4) (*The sign of Jonah.*)

THINK

How long did Jonah spend inside the big fish? (*3 days*) Jesus was going to die on the cross. How long would His body be inside the tomb? (*3 days*) What would happen then? (*He would come back to life.*) Wow! What an amazing sign!

PRAY

Jesus had already given many miraculous signs pointing to who He is. (*Check your display to see some of them.*) But the Pharisees <u>refused</u> to believe them. We're reading about those signs in Matthew's book. Ask God to help <u>you</u> to believe them.

Building up
It seems strange that Jesus refuses to give a sign to who He is. But look again at **verse 1**. Why did they ask for a sign? (*To test/trap Jesus.*) Jesus had spoken about the sign of Jonah already. **Read Matthew 12v38-41** When the people of Nineveh heard Jonah's message, they repented. But these Pharisees had already decided <u>not</u> to believe in Jesus. They just wanted to test Him. That's why Jesus didn't give them a sign.

DAY 36
Spreading lies

KEYPOINT
Jesus warns His followers about the teaching of the religious leaders—spreading like yeast.

Today's passages are:
Table Talk: Matthew 16v5-7 & 11-12
XTB: Matthew 16v5-12

TABLE TALK

Look at some bread. Describe the look and taste of the outside and inside. Bread is made with **yeast**. What does it do? (*Spreads through the <u>whole</u> loaf to make it rise.*)

READ

Yesterday the Pharisees and Sadducees came to test and trap Jesus. Now Jesus warns His followers about them. **Read Matthew 16v5-7**

TALK

What was Jesus warning about? (v6) (*The yeast of the Pharisees and Sadducees.*) But what did the disciples <u>think</u> He was talking about? (v7) (*Bread, because they had forgotten to take any.*) So Jesus reminded them how He had fed huge crowds from almost nothing. Then he explained again.
Read Matthew 16v11-12

What was Jesus warning about? (v12) (*The <u>teaching</u> of the religious leaders.*)

THINK

Wrong teaching, from religious leaders who wouldn't believe Jesus, was spreading everywhere—like yeast. The disciples mustn't believe it.

PRAY

Ask God to help you to spot wrong teaching, and to only believe <u>truth</u> about Jesus.

Building up
Read the full passage in **Matthew 16v5-12** Yet again the disciples were worrying about having no bread—just as they did in v33. Why shouldn't they worry? (*Jesus can provide bread.*) They needed to remember **who** Jesus is, and to trust Him. So do we. Pray that you would **trust** Jesus to look after you.

DAY 37
Jesus jigsaw

KEYPOINT
God shows Peter that Jesus is the Christ (Messiah) —God's chosen King.

Today's passages are:
Table Talk: Matthew 16v13-17
XTB: Matthew 16v13-20

TABLE TALK
Do a very simple child's jigsaw together, but hide one piece. What do you think the missing piece looks like? (*If you have time, it would be fun to try drawing it.*)

READ
Matthew has been building up a picture for us of **who Jesus is**. But the disciples couldn't put the picture together, until, suddenly, Peter slotted in the final piece. **Read Matthew 16v13-17**

TALK
"Son of Man" is a title for Jesus. Who did people think Jesus was? (v14) (*John the Baptist, or an Old T prophet [messenger] such as Elijah or Jeremiah.*) But who does Peter say Jesus is? (v16) (*The Christ/Messiah, the Son of God.*) Who showed this to Peter? (v17) (*God*)

THINK
Christ is a Greek word. **Messiah** is Hebrew. They both mean "God's chosen King." In the Old Testament, God promised His people a **King** who would **rescue** them. Jesus is this King!

DO
Add **"Jesus is the Christ, God's chosen King"** to the "Who is Jesus?" display.

PRAY
Thank God for keeping His promise to send Jesus as our King.

Building up
Read Matthew 16v17-20 What is Jesus going to build? (v18) (*His church.*) This means that many people will believe (they'll be called the church). The name Peter means "rock". Verse 19 probably means that Peter will teach the new Christians what pleases Jesus. (Bind=forbid, loose=permit.)

DAY 38
Royal rescue

KEYPOINT
King Jesus came to suffer and die.

Today's passages are:
Table Talk: Matthew 16v21-23
XTB: Matthew 16v21-23

TABLE TALK
What would you most like about being King or Queen?

READ
The disciples have just learnt that Jesus is God's promised King. Now Jesus tells them what that will mean.
Read Matthew 16v21-23

TALK
Where must Jesus go? (v21) (*Jerusalem*) What will happen in Jerusalem? (v21) (*Jesus will suffer and die.*) What did Peter do when he heard this? (v22) (*He told Jesus off!*) Peter was shocked! He didn't want Jesus to die. But this time Peter was wrong. Where did his ideas come from? (v23) (*From human ideas, rather than God's plans.*) Note: Jesus doesn't mean that Peter is Satan—but that Peter's ideas come from Satan, not God.

DO
Add **"Jesus came to die."** to your "Why did Jesus come?" display.

Explain in your own words <u>why</u> Jesus had to suffer and die. (*He died in our place, to take the punishment for our sins, so that we can be forgiven.*)
Add **"Jesus died to rescue us."** to your "Why did Jesus come?" display.

PRAY
Thank God that Jesus died to rescue you.

Building up
In yesterday's reading, we saw that Jesus is the King. But He is the King who came to die! He came as our *Servant King*. Read Jesus' words in **Mark 10v45**. Praise King Jesus for coming to rescue you.

DAY 39
Follow the leader

KEYPOINT
Following Jesus is hard, but best. He gives eternal life to those who follow Him.

Today's passages are:
Table Talk: Matthew 16v24-25
XTB: Matthew 16v24-28

TABLE TALK

Play a quick game of "Follow the Leader". (*The others have to follow whatever actions the leader makes.*)

READ

The disciples have discovered *who Jesus is*—He's the King. And *what Jesus will do*—He will suffer and die. Now they find out what it means to *follow Him*.
Read Matthew 16v24-25

TALK

What did Jesus say His followers must do? (v24) (*Deny/forget yourself, carry your cross.*)

THINK

If we are to deny ourselves, does that mean we please ourselves or please Jesus? (*Please Jesus, by putting Him first instead of ourselves.*)
If you saw someone carrying a cross in those days, where would they be going? (*To be crucified.*) Jesus' followers had to live **for Him**. For some of them that would mean dying for Him too. Does that mean putting Jesus first in <u>some</u> things or in <u>all</u> things?

Following Jesus is <u>hard</u>. It means doing what Jesus did. It means putting God first, just as Jesus Himself did, even when that leads to suffering. But see how it works out in the end—**read v25**. Jesus gives <u>eternal life</u> to those who follow Him!

PRAY

Ask God to help you follow Jesus in all things, even when that's hard.

Building up
Read Matthew 16v26-28 These verses are hard to understand, but one thing is clear (v26). Living **forever** with Jesus is far better than owning the whole world! Add **"Jesus gives eternal life to those who follow Him"** to your display.

DAY 40
Peak preview

KEYPOINT
The transfiguration showed Peter, James and John who Jesus is. They must listen to Him.

Today's passages are:
Table Talk: Matthew 17v1-8
XTB: Matthew 17v1-8

TABLE TALK

<u>Either:</u> Look at a Transformer (*A toy that changes from a robot to something else*) <u>Or:</u> Think of some words beginning with "trans" e.g. translate (*change into a new language*), transform (*change how it looks*), transfer (*change to a new team*).

READ

Jesus took three of His followers up a mountain. There He was **transfigured** (His appearance changed).
Read Matthew 17v1-8

TALK

How did Jesus change? (*See v2*) Who appeared with Jesus? (v3) (*Moses and Elijah—who both served God in the Old T.*) Then God's voice spoke from a cloud. What <u>four</u> things did God say about Jesus? (v5) (*Jesus is God's Son. God loves Him. God is pleased with Him. The disciples must listen to Jesus.*)

Six days earlier, Jesus had told His disciples something they found hard to believe. What was it? (*That Jesus must die—v21, Day 38.*) Now God is telling them that they must <u>listen</u> to Jesus and <u>believe</u> what He says.

PRAY

The transfiguration gives us a glimpse of how **great** Jesus is. This great King came to die for you! Thank Him!

Building up
God told the disciples to **listen** to Jesus. What do you think that means? (To use their ears? To ignore Him? To think about what He says? To believe Him? To obey Him?) How can <u>you</u> listen to Jesus? Ask God to help you to listen to Jesus and do what He says.

DAY 41
Top secret

KEYPOINT
Jesus warned His disciples not to say who He was, because people wanted the wrong kind of King.

Today's passages are:
Table Talk: Matthew 17v9
XTB: Matthew 17v9-13

TABLE TALK

Imagine living in Israel at the time of Jesus. The Roman army had invaded and taken over the country. The Romans made the rules. Everyone had to obey them. How would you feel about the Romans? If you knew that God had sent you a king, what kind of king would you want him to be?

READ

The Jewish people were waiting for the promised King (the Christ). They wanted him to get rid of the Romans for them. Peter, James and John knew that **Jesus** was the King. They could tell the people all about Him. **Read Matthew 17v9**

TALK

What did Jesus tell them not to do? (Not to tell anyone about Him—see 16v20 as well.) When could they tell everyone? (After Jesus had risen from the dead.)

THINK

Many people had the wrong idea about Jesus. They thought He'd come to rescue them from the Romans. But Jesus came to rescue us from the real problem—**sin**.

PRAY

Many people today have the wrong idea about Jesus too. They think He wasn't special, or didn't even exist. **Pray for your friends.** Ask God to help you to tell them about King Jesus, who came to rescue them.

Building up
Read Matthew 17v10-13 In the Old T, God promised that a prophet like Elijah would come just before the rescuing King. Who was he? (v13) (John the Baptist) How would Jesus be treated like John the Baptist? (John was arrested and killed [Mt 14v1-12, Day 27]. The same would happen to Jesus.)

DAY 42
Power supply

KEYPOINT
The disciples couldn't drive out the demon, because they didn't have faith.

Today's passages are:
Table Talk: Matthew 17v18-20
XTB: Matthew 17v14-23

TABLE TALK

Flashback: Look up **Matthew 10v1** to see what Jesus had told His disciples to do. (To drive out demons and to heal.)

READ

But while Jesus was up the mountain with Peter, James and John, a man came to the other disciples for help. The man's son had a demon, which made the boy ill. The disciples had tried to help, but they couldn't. When Jesus heard about this, He told them to bring the boy to Him. **Read Matthew 17v18-20**

TALK

Did Jesus heal the boy? (v18) (Yes) Why couldn't the disciples heal him? (v20) (They didn't have faith.) The disciples should have trusted Jesus' power and authority. What is possible for people who have faith? (v20) (Everything.)

Jesus had told the disciples to drive out demons, but they didn't have enough faith to do it. They should have trusted in His power to help them.

PRAY

Some of the things God tells us to do may seem impossible. (Like telling others about Him, always being truthful, sharing with people we don't like.) But we can always trust in God's great power to help us to do what He says. Ask Him for that trust.

Building up
Jesus had already given His disciples authority to drive out demons and to heal. And they did. **Read Mark 6v12-13** At that time the disciples could drive out demons, but not now. What was the difference? (Their lack of faith, v20). Jesus' power hadn't changed, but their faith needed to grow, as they learnt new things about Him. In particular, they needed to believe what Jesus had told them about coming to die. Ask God to help your faith grow as you learn new things about Jesus.

DAY 43
Fishy money

KEYPOINT
Jesus is God's Son.

Today's passages are:
Table Talk: Matthew 17v24-27
XTB: Matthew 17v24-27

TABLE TALK

(*You need paper, pencil & a small coin.*)
Draw a large fish with its mouth open.
Take turns to toss the coin into the mouth.

READ

Today Jesus is asked to pay the **temple tax**, which was money collected for the temple. Jesus does pay—but He gets the money from a very surprising place!
Read Matthew 17v24-27

Note: v25 & 28 should say "sons"—not "citizens" as in the Good News Bible.

THINK

Jesus' story about kings and taxes was to help Peter understand that Jesus didn't have to pay the temple tax. He asked Peter, "Who do kings collect money from? Their sons or other people?" What was Peter's answer? (v26) (*Other people.*) Sons don't pay their fathers! A modern equivalent might be a theme park. Who pays to enter a theme park? The owner's son or the general public? (*The public. The son isn't asked to pay.*)

Jesus is <u>God's Son</u>. It was crazy to ask Him to pay for the temple. It belonged to His Father! But Jesus did pay. Where did He get the money from? (v27) (*A fish!*)

DO

Add **"Jesus is God's Son"** to your "Who is Jesus?" display.

PRAY

Jesus is God's Son. Think of some other names for Him. (*King, Rescuer, Friend...*) Praise and thank Jesus for who He is.

Building up
Look up some other verses from Matthew that show that Jesus is God's Son. E.g.
Matthew 3v17, 14v33, 16v16, 17v5
Choose one to copy, and add to your display.

DAY 44-45
Notes for Parents

THE UNFORGIVING SERVANT
We end this part of Matthew with the parable of the Unforgiving Servant. This is a great story to remind your children (and you?) of God's astounding forgiveness, and of how we should respond to that.

ACT IT OUT
This story is great fun to act out. Someone needs to be the King (a crown helps if you have one), someone else the main servant (wearing an apron?), and (if possible) a third person to be the other servant. (If there are only two of you, you can still act it by pretending the existence of the other servant.)

GOING TO EXTREMES
A key part of this parable is the extreme contrast between the amounts of money owed by each servant. The first servant owed ten thousand talents. A talent was the highest unit of currency, and 10,000 the highest Greek number. It's like saying "billions"! In contrast, the second servant owed a few hundred denarii, which is equivalent to just a few pounds.

If possible, find some visual way to show this contrast. For example, use a very long roll of foil or computer paper for the huge amount, and a tiny scrap of paper for the other.

Note: Jesus' teaching about our need to forgive others is hard. It will help your children if they know that you find forgiving others hard too. Like Peter, we can think that forgiving someone seven times is unduly generous of us! We all need to be reminded of God's awesome forgiveness, and what it cost Him...

DAY 44
Royal pardon

KEYPOINT
God forgives all our sin, without limit.

Today's passages are:
Table Talk: Matthew 18v23-27
XTB: Matthew 18v21-27

 TABLE TALK

How easy is it to forgive someone? (*E.g. if they break a promise, or tell lies.*)

Peter thought he should forgive someone **seven** times, but Jesus told him there should be **no limit**. (*This is in v21-22.*) Then Jesus told a story to explain why.

See **Notes for Parents** on the previous page for acting out ideas.

 READ

Act out part one of the story as you read **Matthew 18v23-27**.
(*Part two is tomorrow.*)

 TALK

How much money did the servant owe? (*See v24*) This was a HUGE amount! Could he pay it back? (v25) (*No!*) So what did the king say would happen? (*The servant and his family would be slaves.*) What did the man say to the king? (v26) (*"Be patient with me and I will pay you back."*) What did the king do? (v27) (*The king let him go. He didn't have to pay anything.*)

 THINK

The king in the story is like **God**. The servant is like **us**. The money the servant owes is like **sin**. How much of our sin does God forgive? (*All of it!*) Why? (*Because Jesus died as our Rescuer.*)

 PRAY

If we put our trust in Jesus, God forgives all of our sin, without limit, because Jesus died for us. Thank Him now.

Building up
Read v 26-27 again The servant said that he would pay back the debt, but it wasn't possible. The amount was too much. It's not possible for **us** to solve the problem of our own sin either. Only Jesus can do that. Thank Jesus for dying to rescue you from sin.

DAY 45
Royal rebuke

KEYPOINT
Because God forgives us without limit, we should forgive others without limit too.

Today's passages are:
Table Talk: Matthew 18v28-35
XTB: Matthew 18v28-35

 TABLE TALK

Recap yesterday's story.

 READ

Act out part two of the story as you read **Matthew 18v28-35**

 TALK

The first servant had just been let off a HUGE amount of money. Then he met another servant who owed him just a few pounds. What did he do? (v28) (*Grabbed the man and demanded his money.*) Could the second servant pay? (*No*) So what did the first servant do? (v30) (*Threw him into prison.*)

 THINK

How different is that from the way the king had treated him? (*Very different!*) What should the first servant have done and why? (*Cancelled the debt, just as the king had cancelled his debt.*)

This story seems to be about money, but it's really about forgiveness. God has forgiven **us** without limit. So what should we do? (*Forgive others without limit too*)

 PRAY

Thank God for His forgiveness. Ask Him to help you forgive others too.

Building up
Talk more about what it means to forgive someone. Does it mean pretending they haven't hurt us? When is it right to tell others about someone hurting us? (*E.g. if being bullied.*) What should we do if someone says sorry to us? Really forgiving someone is hard (for adults as well as children!). Ask God to help you.

DAY 46-65
Notes for Parents

WHO'S THE BOSS?

Draw a crown and write "Who is King?" under it. Stick it somewhere you will see while reading Exodus.

This is the BIG question in Exodus. Pharaoh thinks that he is the most important person around. He is, after all, king of the hugely powerful country of Egypt. But he needs to learn the real truth—that **God** is King!

THE STORY SO FAR...

- The Israelites are **slaves** in Egypt.
- God has promised to **rescue** them.
- He has chosen **Moses** to be their leader.

THE LAST STRAW...

The Israelites worked very hard making bricks for the Egyptians. But Pharaoh decided that they were lazy, and gave new instructions to their slave drivers...

Don't give the Israelites straw any more. Make them get their own!

But make sure they make just as many bricks as before!

So the Israelites searched all over Egypt for straw. ...this made their work slower...

Where are today's bricks? You haven't done enough! Why not?

The Israelite foremen went to see Pharaoh. It's not our fault! We can't make bricks without straw!

But Pharaoh refused to help. You're lazy! You won't be given any straw!

DAY 46 Grasping at straws

KEYPOINT
God is the real King. But Pharaoh doesn't know this yet and refuses to obey God.

Today's passages are:
Table Talk: Exodus 5v1-2
XTB: Exodus 5v1-21

TABLE TALK

Read *"Who's the Boss?"* together in **Notes for Parents**, and make the "Who is King?" poster.

Then use *"The Story So Far..."* to recap the first part of the book of Exodus.

READ

Moses and his brother Aaron went to see Pharaoh. They had a message from God. **Read Exodus 5v1-2**

TALK

What was God's message to Pharaoh? (v1) (*"Let my people go."*) Who does God mean by "my people"? (*The Israelites.*) But Pharaoh was very proud. What was his answer? (*See v2*)

Pharaoh was angry that the Israelites wanted to leave, so he made their work even harder. Read *"The Last Straw"* and cartoon in **Notes for Parents**.

THINK

It wasn't fair! Now the Israelites had to work even harder. It <u>looked</u> like Pharaoh could do what he liked. He seemed to be in charge of everything. But he wasn't! He was about to find out that **God** is the <u>real</u> King!

PRAY

The book of Exodus shows us that God is the **King of Kings**. Ask God to help you to get to know Him better as you read Exodus together.

Building up

Making bricks without straw was unfair. How do you think the Israelites felt? **Read verses 19-21** to see what they did. Who did they blame? (*Moses*) Things had got worse for the Israelites. Did this mean God couldn't keep His promise to save them? Why/why not? (*Think about what you know about God's character.*) We'll find out more about this tomorrow.

DAY 47
A broken promise?

KEYPOINT
Nothing can stop God's plans. He is always in control.

Today's passages are:
Table Talk: Exodus 6v1-8
XTB: Exodus 5v22-6v8

TABLE TALK

Recap yesterday's story. How had things got worse for the Israelites? (*They had to make just as many bricks, but with no straw.*)

Moses found it hard to understand why God hadn't rescued the Israelites yet, and why things were getting worse.

But God hadn't forgotten His promises. He said to Moses, **"Now you will see what I will do."** (Ex 6v1)

READ

As you read the passage, tell your child to listen for the words "I will". Every time they hear them, they must stand up, turn around and sit down again.
Read Exodus 6v1-8

TALK

How many times did you stand up? God promised some amazing things. He said He would bring them out of Egypt (v6), free them from slavery (v6) and give them the promised land of Canaan (v8).

THINK

Why didn't God say "I'm hoping to..." or "I'll probably..."? (*Nothing can stop His plans, His words are always true.*)

PRAY

Even when things look bad, nothing and no-one can stop God's plans. Thank Him that He is always in control.

Building up
Talk about anything that you are worried about at the moment, or finding hard. Things <u>looked</u> like they were getting worse for the Israelites, but as we read through Exodus we will see that God was always in control. His plans were working out perfectly. Thank God that He is always in control. Ask Him to help you to trust Him, even when that's hard.

DAY 48
God's mighty hand

KEYPOINT
God's will stretch out His hand to show that He is the LORD, the real King.

Today's passages are:
Table Talk: Exodus 7v5
XTB: Exodus 6v28-7v5

TABLE TALK

Each draw around your hand. Keep the drawing for later.

READ

As we saw yesterday, God has promised Moses that He **will** rescue the Israelites. But Moses is still worried. "Why would Pharaoh listen to me?", he asked. God told Moses that his brother Aaron would speak for him. God also said that He would do mighty acts to show Pharaoh who really is King.
Read Exodus 7v5

TALK

What will the Egyptians know? (*That God is the LORD.*) How? (*God will stretch out His hand against Egypt, and rescue the Israelites.*) This doesn't mean a giant hand in the sky! What does it mean? (*God will show His great power.*)

Copy v5 onto the largest hand. Write **"God is King"** on the other hands.

PRAY

Thank God that He is the King of Kings.

Building up
Read the full passage in **Exodus 6v28-7v5** God tells Moses what's about to happen in the next nine chapters of Exodus! What will happen? (*Aaron will speak for Moses, Pharaoh's heart will be hard and he won't listen, God will do miraculous signs and wonders, and rescue the Israelites.*) As these things happen, the Egyptians will see that God is the LORD, the real King. Ask God to help <u>you</u> to see that too.

DAY 49
Sticks and snakes

(*You each need paper and pencil.*)

Flashback: Ask your child to **draw** the answer to each question. **1**—When God first spoke to Moses, what did He speak from? (*The burning bush*) **2**—God gave Moses three signs to show he had been sent by God. Draw what happened when Moses threw down his staff. (*It turned into a snake.*)

God had also told Moses that Pharaoh would <u>not</u> listen to him. Read the passage to see what happened.
Read Exodus 7v6-13

How old was Moses? (v6) (*80*) What happened to Aaron's staff? (v10) (*It became a snake.*) Were Pharaoh's magicians able to do the same thing? (v12) (*Yes*) But what happened to their snakes? (*Aaron's staff swallowed them!*)

God had told Moses that Pharaoh wouldn't listen to him. Was He right? (*Yes*) Which words in v13 show that? (*"Just as the LORD had said."*)

Thank God that His words always come true.

Building up
Read v11-12 again. For a moment it looked like the magicians were just as powerful as God. But then what happened? (*Aaron's staff swallowed theirs!*) Later, when we read about the plagues, the magicians will be able to copy the first two plagues. But then they give up (Ex 8v18-19). It became clear to them, and hopefully to us too as we read Exodus, that **nobody** is as powerful as God.

DAY 50
Patterns, plagues and prayers

 TABLE TALK

For the next ten days we're going to be reading about the plagues. Use **Notes for Parents** (on the next page) to find out about the <u>pattern</u> of the plagues, and what they show about God. If you can, make a poster as suggested.

 READ

God told Moses what the plagues would show. Read both passages, looking out for the repeated words or ideas.
Read Exodus 7v17 & 10v1-2

What were the repeated words/ideas? (*"You will know that I am the Lord."*)

 THINK

Do you remember what the BIG question is in the book of Exodus? (*"Who is King?"*) God is going to use the plagues to show the Egyptians the answer to this question. He is going to show them that <u>He</u> is the King of Kings.

 PRAY

Pharaoh and the Egyptians needed to know that God is the LORD, the King of Kings. So do many countries today. Each day we will pray for one country, and ask God to show the people and leaders of that country that <u>He</u> is the real King. Use the **World Prayer** box at the bottom of the page.

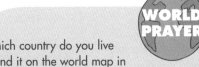

Which country do you live in? Find it on the world map in **Notes for Parents**.

Pray for the leaders of your country. Ask God to help them to make good and fair decisions. Ask God to help them to understand that He is the King of Kings, and that the Bible will show them the best was to lead the country.

Notes for Parents

PATTERN PLAGUES

As we saw yesterday, Pharaoh refused to listen to God's message. So now God would send **ten plagues** on Egypt—ten terrible miracles. The first nine plagues came in a **pattern**. They came in three triplets. Each triplet showed something amazing about God.

Plagues 1, 2 & 3 ⟶ You can't beat **God**.

Plagues 4, 5 & 6 ⟶ The Israelites are **God's** people.

Plagues 7, 8 & 9 ⟶ **God** is the GREATEST.

Look out for this pattern over the next few days.

1 2 3 ⟶ You can't beat God

4 5 6 ⟶ The Israelites are God's people

7 8 9 ⟶ God is the GREATEST

MAKE A POSTER

We will be looking at this pattern of plagues over the next ten days. It will help you if you make a poster of this pattern, and put it somewhere where you will see it each day.

Your children may like to draw a pattern around the edge, design one on a computer, or use thumbprints, stickers or rubber stamps.

World Map

DAY 51
One two three

KEYPOINT
The first three plagues were of blood, frogs and gnats.

Today's passages are:
Table Talk: Exodus 7v20-24
XTB: Exodus 7v20-24

TABLE TALK

(*You need a world atlas.*) Look up Egypt in an atlas, and find the river Nile.

The Nile is the biggest river in Egypt. Early one morning, God sent Moses and Aaron to the Nile to meet Pharaoh. They went to warn Pharaoh about the first plague. **Read Exodus 7v20-24**

READ

What happened to the Nile? (v20-21) (*It's water turned to blood, the fish died and it smelt really bad.*) Where did the Egyptians get their water? (v24) (*They dug along the river bank.*) Did Pharaoh listen to Moses? (v22) (*No*)

TALK

The next two plagues were terrible too. **Frogs** came pouring out of the Nile, and hopped everywhere. Then in the third plague, the dust turned into crawling, biting **gnats** that covered the people and animals.

More about these plagues tomorrow. *Today, use the World Prayer section to pray for modern Egypt.*

PRAY

WORLD PRAYER

The Capital of modern **Egypt** is Cairo. It is the largest city in Africa. About half the people in Cairo are very poor and live in slums.

Thank God for the Christians who go into the slums to help the poor. **Ask God** to help them show the poor that God loves them and that He is their real King.

DAY 52
You can't beat God!

KEYPOINT
Pharaoh's magicians tried to compete with God—but they couldn't. No-one can beat God.

Today's passages are:
Table Talk: Exodus 8v8-15
XTB: Exodus 8v8-19

TABLE TALK

Cut out an outline of a frog. Use a newspaper to flap the frog into different places e.g. under the table, through a doorway, under a chair...

READ

In the second plague, frogs poured out of the river Nile. They went everywhere—into the houses, the beds and even the ovens! They were all over the people too. Then Pharaoh asked Moses for help. **Read Exodus 8v8-15**

TALK

What two things did Pharaoh say to Moses? (v8) (*Pray to God to take the frogs away, then he will let the people go.*) Moses said the frogs would leave at a time chosen by Pharaoh. Why? (v10) (*So he would know there is no-one like God.*) When the frogs had gone, did Pharaoh let the people go? (v15) (*No*)

Pharaoh's magicians were able to copy the first two plagues—blood and frogs. But in the third plague, the dust was turned into **gnats**. This time, the magicians couldn't do it. They told Pharaoh that **God** had created the gnats, (v19) but Pharaoh still wouldn't listen.

More tomorrow...

WORLD PRAYER

The river Nile runs through **Sudan**, a country that has been hit by war and famine for many years. One result of the long war is that Christians have had to move all around the country. Pray for these Christians. **Ask God** to help them to keep following Jesus, even when that's very hard, and to tell other people about Jesus too.

DAY 53
Four five six

Today's passages are:
Table Talk: Exodus 8v20-24
XTB: Exodus 8v20-24

 TABLE TALK
Tell each other Waiter jokes or fly jokes. E.g. "Waiter, waiter! What's this fly doing in my soup? Is it backstroke, Sir?"

 READ
The next plague was worse than having twenty flies in your soup!
Read Exodus 8v20-24

 TALK
When did Moses speak to Pharaoh? (v20) (*Early in the morning.*) Where did God say the flies would go? (v21) (*On Pharaoh, his officials, on the Egyptians and in their houses.*) Where did the flies not go? (v22) (*Goshen, where the Israelites lived, see the map below.*)

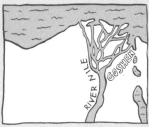

 THINK
Check your poster from Day 50. What did the first three plagues show? (*You can't beat God.*) What will these next three plagues show? (*The Israelites are God's special people.*)

WORLD PRAYER

Find Papua New Guinea on the map in Notes for Parents for Day 50. There are over 800 different groups of people living in **Papua New Guinea** (PNG), and each group speaks its own language! Everyone also speaks "Tok Pisin", a kind of simple English. My friend Rosie works in PNG as a doctor. She also teaches women there about Jesus, and helps them understand the Bible.
Pray for Rosie, and other Christian missionaries in PNG. **Ask God** to help them to tell people the great news about Jesus.

DAY 54
God's special people

Today's passages are:
Table Talk: Exodus 9v1-7
XTB: Exodus 9v1-7

 TABLE TALK
Recap: What was yesterday's plague? (*Flies*) Where did the flies go? (*Where the Egyptians lived.*) Where didn't they go? (*Goshen, where the Israelites live*)

 READ
God then warned Pharaoh what would happen if he didn't let the Israelites go.
Read Exodus 9v1-5

 TALK
What would this plague be? (*All the Egyptian animals would die, but not t* Israelites animals.*) Do you think Phara will obey God this time? (*Discuss what you think and why.*)

Read Exodus 9v6-7

Pharaoh didn't listen, so God's words came true. How many of the Egyptian animals died? (v6) (*All*) Pharaoh sent men to check the Israelite animals. How many of those animals died? (v7) (*Nor*)

 THINK
Plague six was a plague of **boils**. (v8-12) Who do you think did get boils? (T *Egyptians*) Who didn't? (The *Israelites*)

In each plague, God clearly showed Pharaoh that the Israelites were different from the Egyptians. They were **God's** special people.

WORLD PRAYER

Haiti is the poorest country in the western world. Many people practice voodoo, which involves worshipping spirits. It often leaves people full o fear. One way the people hear about Jesus is through Christian radio stations. **Ask God** to help people in Haiti to understand what they h on the Christian radio stations, and to learn about God's love for them.

DAY 55
Seven eight nine

KEYPOINT
The next three plagues were hail, locusts and darkness. They showed that God is the greatest.

Today's passages are:
Table Talk: Exodus 9v13-19
XTB: Exodus 9v13-19

TABLE TALK

I was once in a hailstorm so strong it nearly knocked me off my bike! Talk about any hailstorms you've been in, or close your eyes and try to imagine one.

READ

God warned Pharaoh that the next plague would be the **worst hailstorm** that had ever hit Egypt.
Read Exodus 9v13-19

Check your poster from Day 50 to see what plagues 7, 8 and 9 showed. (*God is the Greatest.*) God was going to show He is the greatest by sending the **worst hailstorm** ever, **more locusts** than ever before, and then making it **so dark** that the darkness could be felt!

TALK

God told Pharaoh <u>why</u> these plagues were happening. Why? (v14) (*"So that you may know there is <u>no-one</u> like me in all the earth."*) God even said that <u>He</u> had made Pharaoh king of Egypt so that everyone in the world would know about God and His power! (v16) *Tomorrow we'll see how Pharaoh reacts.*

PRAY

India is a country where the people need to know about the <u>one great God</u>. Find it on your world map, then use the prayer below.

WORLD PRAYER

India is full of temples and shrines. The people are very religious. Most are Hindus, but there are many other religions too. Christian missionaries have worked in India for hundreds of years. But now it is hard for missionaries from other countries to get visas to work in India, so today most missionaries are Indians. Pray for these Indian Christians. **Ask God** to help them to tell others the great news about the <u>one God</u>, who loves them.

DAY 56
God's the greatest

KEYPOINT
Some of Pharaoh's officials obeyed God, but Pharaoh still refused to obey God.

Today's passages are:
Table Talk: Exodus 9v19-21
XTB: Exodus 9v15-21

TABLE TALK

Recap: What did plagues seven, eight and nine show? (*God is the greatest.*)

READ

Pharaoh and his officials had the warnings about the plagues. They could choose to <u>obey</u> God, or <u>ignore</u> Him. Read more about the plague of hail to see how Pharaoh and his officials reacted. **Read Exodus 9v19-21**

TALK

Some of Pharaoh's officials <u>believed</u> God's words. What did they do? (v20) (*Brought their slaves and animals inside.*) Others <u>ignored</u> God. What did they do? (v21) (*Left everything outside.*)

The hail did come—just as God had said—and all those left outside were killed.

THINK

After each plague, Pharaoh had a choice to make. He could **obey** God, and let the Israelites go, or he could **ignore** God. Sometimes Pharaoh refused even to listen to God. Sometimes (like after the hail) he said he would let the Israelites go—**read v28**.
<u>BUT</u> once the plague stopped, he changed his mind again—**read v35**.

Pharaoh still needed to learn that God really is the King of Kings...

WORLD PRAYER

You may have seen **Romania** in the news. When the government changed there a few years ago, there were many news reports about the thousands of children living in orphanages. **Pray** that those children have the love and care they need. Pray too for the many Christians who teach the children about God.

DAY 57
Hard hearted

KEYPOINT
Pharaoh's heart was hard, so God warned him about the final plague, the death of the firstborn.

Today's passages are:
Table Talk: Exodus 11v1-8
XTB: Exodus 11v1-8

Each draw a heart. Now make it look hard by covering it in armour plating, or drawing a "No Entry" sign on it.

Pharaoh's heart was **hard**. He wouldn't listen to Moses & didn't care about God.

(If you have time, look at how this started with Pharaoh hardening his heart himself [Ex 8v15 & 32], but that later God hardened Pharaoh's heart [Ex 10v20 & 27]. God made Pharaoh what he had already <u>chosen</u> to be.)

Pharaoh's heart was now rock hard. But the last plague would change everything.

Read Exodus 11v1-8

After this last plague, what would Pharaoh do? (v1) (*Drive them out of Egypt.*) This would be a terrible plague. The eldest son (the firstborn) of every <u>Egyptian</u> family would die. So would the firstborn of all the Egyptian cattle. But the eldest sons of the <u>Israelites</u> would be kept safe. *We'll find out more about this in the next few days.*

WORLD PRAYER

The plagues showed God's great power to the Egyptians. They saw that He is the LORD—the King of Kings.

*Turn to the World Map in **Notes for Parents** on Day 50.*

Our world is full of people who don't know that God is their LORD. Some have hardened their hearts, like Pharaoh. Other have never even heard about the one true God who loves them.
But there are also <u>Christians</u> living in every country of the world. **Ask God** to help those Christians, wherever they live, to tell others about Jesus. Ask God to help <u>you</u> to tell your friends about Jesus too.

DAY 58
Passover

KEYPOINT
God told the Israelites exactly how to prepare for the final plague, the Passover.

Today's passages are:
Table Talk: Exodus 12v5-13
XTB: Exodus 12v1-13

TABLE TALK
Each person has one minute to find an item of clothing you wear for a special activity. (E.g. football boots, swimsuit...)

READ
In today's verses, the Israelites are told to dress in <u>travelling clothes</u> (with a cloak and staff). But then they stay <u>inside</u> for a meal! At the meal they are to eat roast lamb. **Read Exodus 12v5-11**

TALK
Before cooking the lamb, what are they to do with the blood? (v7) (*Put it on the sides and tops of the doorframes.*) They are to eat the lamb roasted—not raw or boiled. How are they to be dressed? (See v11)

Read Exodus 12v12-13

THINK
That night, God will pass through Egypt. Every firstborn son and animal will die. This final plague is called **Passover**. Why? (*When God see the blood on the doorposts of a house, He will **pass over** that house.*) The blood marked where the Israelites lived. Everyone inside those houses would be kept safe.

God told the Israelites exactly what to do to stay safe. Do you think they will obey Him? Why/why not? (*More tomorrow.*)

PRAY
Obeying God is <u>always</u> the best and safest thing to do. Ask God to help you obey Him, even when that's hard.

Building up
Read Exodus 12v1-5 List all the things these verses tell you about the Passover lamb. God said the lamb must be **perfect** (v5). It would die in place of the eldest son. Does this remind you of anyone? (*Jesus who was perfect, died in our place, so that we can be saved.*) More about this in the next two days...

The Passover lamb

> **KEYPOINT**
>
> The Passover lamb died in the place of the eldest son, who was kept safe.
>
> Today's passages are:
> **Table Talk:** Exodus 12v28-30
> **XTB:** Exodus 12v21-30

BLE LK

Play a quick game of **hangman**. The word to guess is "doorframe".

What did God tell the Israelites to do to their doorframes? (*Put lamb's blood on the top and sides.*)

AD

God has told the Israelites exactly how to stay safe during the Passover. But they must obey Him.
Read Exodus 12v28-30

Did the Israelites obey God? (v28) (*Yes*) What happened at midnight? (v29) (*The eldest son of every Egyptian died.*)

NK

That night something or someone died in **every house**. Who died in the Egyptian homes? (v29) (*The oldest son.*) What died in the Israelite homes? (*The Passover lamb.*) In the Israelite homes the oldest son was kept safe. The Passover lamb died instead, in his place. *More about this tomorrow.*

AY

The Passover happened **just as God had said**. And the Israelites were kept safe **just as God had said**. Thank God that His words always come true.

Building up

God told the Israelites that they were to celebrate the Passover every year from now on. **Read Exodus 12v24-27** Who were they to tell about the Passover? (v26) (*Their children*) Why was it important to tell their children each year? (*So they would grow up knowing how God had kept His promises and rescued His people.*) What can <u>you</u> do to remind yourself that God always keeps His promises?

The lamb of God

> **KEYPOINT**
>
> Like a Passover lamb, Jesus died in our place, as our Rescuer.
>
> Today's passages are:
> **Table Talk:** John 1v29
> **XTB:** John 1v29

TABLE TALK

What date is Christmas Day? (*Dec 25th*) What date is Easter Sunday this year? Will it be the same next year? (*No. It changes each year. Easter Sunday is the first Sunday after the full moon which happens on or after March 21st.*)

The very first **Easter** happened at **Passover** time. (The date of Passover is also set by the moon.) This wasn't by accident! It's because both Easter and Passover are about being **Rescued**.

READ

Today we're jumping into the New Testament to discover something John the Baptist said about Jesus.
Read John 1v29

TALK

What did John call Jesus? (*The lamb of God.*) John was saying that Jesus is like a Passover lamb! When the lamb died at <u>Passover</u> it died **in place of** the eldest son. When Jesus died at <u>Easter</u> (which was also Passover time) He died **in our place**.

DO

Use **Notes for Parents** on the next page to think some more about this.

PRAY

Thank God for sending Jesus to die in our place, so that we can be forgiven.

Building up

In the book of Revelation Jesus looks like a lamb—a Lamb who has been killed. The angels are singing His praises. **Read Revelation 5v12-13** Praise and thank Jesus, the Lamb of God, for dying for you.

THE PASSOVER LAMB

(You need paper, scissors and a red pen.)

Draw some doorposts as shown, and cut them out.

Each Israelite family put the blood from a lamb on the top and sides of their doorframes. *Add red marks to the doorposts.*

In the <u>Egyptian</u> homes, the oldest son died. But in the <u>Israelite</u> homes the eldest son was kept safe. The Passover lamb died instead, in his place. That means the eldest son could say: **"That lamb died instead of me!"**

THE LAMB OF GOD

Jesus was called "the lamb of God". Like a Passover lamb, Jesus died in our place, as our **Rescuer**.

Cut the doorposts as shown, and re-arrange to make a cross.

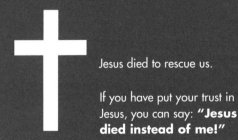

Jesus died to rescue us.

If you have put your trust in Jesus, you can say: **"Jesus died instead of me!"**

"There is the lamb of God, who takes away the sin of the world!"
John 1v29

KEYPOINT
God rescued the Israelites from Egypt, just as He had promised. God always keeps His promise

Today's passages are:
Table Talk: Exodus 12v31-38
XTB: Exodus 12v31-38

TABLE TALK

Imagine you suddenly find you're going on holiday in one minute! Name <u>three things</u> you would take with you.

READ

Right from the beginning of Exodus we seen God's promise that He will rescue the Israelites from Egypt. Now at last i time for them to leave, and they have long journey ahead of them.
Read Exodus 12v31-38

TALK

Pharaoh told the Israelites to leave. W did he tell them to take with them? (v3 (*Their flocks and herds.*) What else di they take? (v34-35) (*Dough without yeast, silver and gold, clothing.*)

Do you remember what the Israelites wore when they ate the Passover meal roast lamb? (*Their travelling clothes— 12v11, Day 58.*) That was because th would be leaving Egypt <u>very soon</u>. No at last they were on their way—just as God had said. God had kept His pron to rescue the Israelites.

PRAY

God <u>always</u> keeps His promises. Than God that He is like this.

Building up

God kept another promise as well. 700 yea before, God had promised Abraham that he would have a HUGE family. So enormous tha trying to count them would be like trying to co all the stars in the sky! **Read Genesis 15v.** How many men left Egypt? (Exodus 12v37) (600,000!) If you add the women and childre there were probably over Two Million Israelite God really had kept His promise to Abraham

Flashback

Pillar case

KEYPOINT
Joseph was sure that God would keep His promise to rescue the Israelites. He was right!

Today's passages are:
Table Talk: Genesis 50v24-26
XTB: Genesis 15v12-14 & 50v24-26

Ask your children what they know about the story of **Joseph**. (*There's a summary in Notes for Parents on Day 16.*)

When Joseph was very old, and still living in Egypt, he told his brothers what he wanted them to do with his body.
Read Genesis 50v24-26

What did Joseph say God would do? (v24) (*Rescue the Israelites and take them back to the promised land of Canaan.*) What did he ask his brothers to do? (v25) (*Promise that Joseph's body would be taken from Egypt back to Canaan.*)

Check out what happened to Joseph's body in **Exodus 13v19**

What did Moses do? (*Take Joseph's body out of Egypt.*)

Joseph was sure God's promise would come true. He was right! Do <u>you</u> believe that God's words always come true? <u>If you do</u>, it's because God has helped you to trust Him. So thank Him. <u>If you're not sure</u>, ask God to help you to believe.

Building up
The Israelites were all the family of one man, Abraham. God had told Abraham what would happen to his family. **Read Genesis 15v12-14** God told Abraham these things 700 years before the time of Moses! Look through the list again. How many of them came true? (*All of them!*)

KEYPOINT
God guided the Israelites with a pillar of cloud by day and fire by night.

Today's passages are:
Table Talk: Exodus 13v20-22
XTB: Exodus 13v17-22

TABLE TALK

When you go somewhere as a family, or on a school trip, how do you make sure no-one gets lost?

READ

When a tourist guide takes visitors through busy streets, he often holds up an umbrella to follow, so they don't get lost. God gave the Israelites something much better to follow!
Read Exodus 13v20-22

TALK

How did God guide them by day? (v21) (*A pillar of cloud.*) How did He guide them at night? (*A pillar of fire.*) Why not cloud all the time? (*It wouldn't show up at night, so they could have got lost.*)

THINK

God guides <u>us</u> too, but in a different way. His word, the Bible, shows us the best way to live for Him. Psalm 119v105 says, **"Your word is a lamp to guide me, and light for my path."**

DO

(*Optional*) Copy this psalm onto some paper, and stick it on the wall.

PRAY

Ask God to guide you as you read His word, the Bible, together. Ask Him to show you the best way to live for Him.

Building up
Read Exodus 13v17-18 Where did God <u>not</u> guide them? (*Through the Philistine country.*) Why not? (*If it looked like they had to fight the Philistines, they might go back to Egypt.*) The route through Philistine country would have been shorter, but God knew what was <u>best</u> for His people. Thank God that He always knows what's best. Ask Him to show you the best way to live for Him.

DAY 64
Making a splash

Today's passages are:
Table Talk : Exodus 14v15-22
XTB : Exodus 14v1-22

TABLE TALK

Note: With young children, it's fun to act this story out. Use two blue sheets or towels for the water, then separate them to make the path across the sea.

The Israelites have escaped from Egypt, but they're not safe yet. Pharaoh has changed his mind again, and is now chasing after them with his whole army, including over 600 chariots! They caught up with the Israelites by the Red Sea.

READ

The Israelites were terrified, but Moses told them not to be afraid. "The LORD will fight for you", he said.
Read Exodus 14v15-22

TALK

What did God tell Moses to do? (*See v16*) What moved between the Israelites and the Egyptian army? (v19) (*The angel of God and the pillar of cloud.*) What happened during the night? (v21-22) (*God divided the waters with an east wind, and they crossed over.*)

DO

Either act the story out, or draw what you think the walls of water looked like.

Talk about how you would have felt as you walked across. What would you think about God?

PRAY

God is just as great today. Praise and thank Him.

Building up
God had done amazing miracles to rescue His people. But the Israelites still found it hard to trust Him. **Read Exodus 14v10-14** Do you find it hard to trust God sometimes, even though you know how powerful He is? Ask Him to help you to "stand firm" (v14), and keep trusting Him, even if you feel scared.

DAY 65
Safe at last?

Today's passages are:
Table Talk : Exodus 14v23-25 & 29-3
XTB : Exodus 14v23-31

TABLE TALK

Recap the story of crossing the Red Se

The Israelites had escaped across the R Sea—but the Egyptians were right beh them! **Read Exodus 14v23-25**

What did God do to the army? (*Conf them, and jammed their chariot whee* What did the Egyptians realise? (v25) (*God was fighting against them.*)

READ

God then sent the waters of the sea ba to their place, and the Egyptian army trapped. The Israelites were safe at las
Read Exodus 14v29-31

TALK

When the Israelites saw God's great power, what did they do? (v31) (*They feared/respected the Lord, and put th trust in Him and in Moses.*)

All through Exodus we've been asking question "Who is King?" What is the answer? (**God** is the real King.)

THINK

Think back over the events in Exodus— how God chose Moses, sent the plagu and rescued His people just as He promised. What have you learnt abou God's character?

PRAY

Praise and thank God for all that you have learnt about Him.

Building up
Now that the Israelites have been rescued, what n they do? Check **Exodus 3v12 & 7v16**. (*They mu worship God.*) So far Exodus had said 16 times that are to worship God! **He** is their true King, so it's righ praise Him and obey Him. The next part of Exodus (i Issue Four of Table Talk) shows if they do or not.

How about you? Will you praise God for being your King? Do you want to obey Him in every part of you life? If you do, then ask Him to help you.

Extra Readings

WHY ARE THERE EXTRA READINGS?

Table Talk and **XTB** both come out every three months. The main Bible reading pages contain material for 65 days. That's enough to use them Monday to Friday for three months.

Many families find that their routine is different at weekends from during the week. Some find that regular Bible reading fits in well on school days, but not at weekends. Others encourage their children to read the Bible for themselves during the week, then explore the Bible together as a family at weekends, when there's more time to do the activities together.

The important thing is to help your children get into the habit of reading the Bible for themselves—and that they see that regular Bible reading is important for **you** as well.

If you **are** able to read the Bible with your children every day, that's great! The extra readings on the next page will augment the main **Table Talk** pages so that you have enough material to cover the full three months.

You could:

- Read **Table Talk** every day for 65 days, then use the extra readings for the rest of the third month.

- Read **Table Talk** on weekdays. Use the extra readings at weekends.

- Use any other combination that works for your family.

PEOPLE OF FAITH

In the Old Testament there are lots of exciting stories about people who had faith in God. Chapter 11 of Hebrews tells us more about their faith—how they trusted God to keep His promises, even when it didn't look like He would.

There are 26 Bible readings on the next page. Part of each verse has been printed for you—but with a word missing. Fill in the missing words as you read the verses. Then see if you can find them all in the wordsearch.

Note: Some are written backwards—or diagonally!!

W	O	R	S	H	I	P	P	E	D	R	A	T	S	A
P	L	E	A	S	E	D	R	S	T	A	R	S	B	B
O	W	F	H	O	P	E	A	N	G	E	L	E	T	R
O	A	U	A	B	C	C	I	T	Y	S	L	O	W	A
R	L	S	V	E	I	L	S	H	E	D	I	E	D	H
E	L	E	E	R	A	C	E	A	N	N	O	A	H	A
V	S	D	E	T	S	E	T	P	U	E	N	S	F	M
O	W	N	G	O	D	S	E	P	T	X	S	H	A	M
S	B	A	H	A	R	A	L	E	H	I	O	E	I	Y
S	E	J	A	C	O	B	Y	N	R	S	U	S	T	D
A	A	S	U	S	E	J	R	T	E	T	L	I	H	O
P	R	O	M	I	S	E	D	O	E	S	E	N	O	B

Extra Readings

1 ☐ **Read Hebrews 11v1-2**

Faith means trusting that God's words in the Bible are true, and that God will keep all His promises.

"Faith is being sure of what we h _ _ _ for." (v1)

2 ☐ **Read Hebrews 11v3**

God created EVERYTHING—just by saying it must be made!

"The universe was created by G _ _ ' word." (v3)

3 ☐ **Read Hebrews 11v4**

Cain & Abel were Adam & Eve's sons. Abel had faith in God, and gave Him the best of his flock as a sacrifice. But Cain was angry, and killed his brother.

"By faith A _ _ _ offered God a better sacrifice than Cain did." (v4)

4 ☐ **Read Hebrews 11v5**

Enoch was Adam's great, great, great, great grandson! Genesis 5 tells us that he "walked with God" for 300 years. Enoch didn't die. God just took him!

"Before Enoch was taken up, he had p _ _ _ _ _ _ God." (v5)

5 ☐ **Read Hebrews 11v6**

The ONLY way to please God is by faith.

"Anyone who comes to God must believe that He e _ _ _ _ _ _ ." (v6)

6 ☐ **Read Hebrews 11v7**

Imagine being told to build a HUGE boat miles from the sea! Noah had faith—and he built the Ark.

"N _ _ _ obeyed God and built an ark to save his family." (v7)

7 ☐ **Read Hebrews 11v8**

God told Abraham to leave his home, his father's family and his country. Abraham trusted and obeyed God.

"By faith A _ _ _ _ _ _ _ obeyed." (v8)

8 ☐ **Read Hebrews 11v9-10**

God made three amazing promises to Abraham, Isaac and Jacob. He promised Land, Children and Blessing. You can find out more about these promises in Notes for Parents on Day 16.

"By faith Abraham lived as a foreigner in the country that God had p _ _ _ _ _ _ _ _ him." (v9)

9 ☐ **Read Hebrews 11v11-12**

Abraham trusted God to give him a son, even though he and Sarah were now too old. God kept His promise!

"His descendants were as numerous as the s _ _ _ _ _ in the sky." (v12)

10 ☐ **Read Hebrews 11v13**

Faith means trusting that God will keep His promises. That's what the people in Hebrews 11 believed.

"All these people were still living by faith when they d _ _ _ ." (v13)

Extra Readings

11 ☐ Read Hebrews 11v14-16
The people in Hebrews 11 were looking forward to being with God in heaven.
"God has prepared a C _ _ _ for them." (v16)

12 ☐ Read Hebrews 11v17-18
God tested Abraham by telling him to kill his own son as a sacrifice. Abraham was willing to do it because he loved God more than anything or anyone else.
"By faith Abraham, when God t _ _ _ _ _ him, offered Isaac as a sacrifice." (v17)

13 ☐ Read Hebrews 11v19
God provided a ram to die in Isaac's place. In the same way, God provided His own Son Jesus to die in our place, so that we can be forgiven. Three days later, God brought Jesus back to life!.
"Abraham reckoned that God could r _ _ _ _ the dead." (v19)

14 ☐ Read Hebrews 11v20
God had made three amazing promises to Abraham. He renewed those promises to Abraham's son Isaac, and his grandson Jacob.
"By faith Isaac blessed J _ _ _ _ and Esau." (v20)

15 ☐ Read Hebrews 11v21
By the time Jacob died he was living in Egypt (not the land God had promised!). But Jacob continued to trust God and to worship Him.
"Jacob leaned on his staff and W _ _ _ _ _ _ _ _ _ _ God."

16 ☐ Read Hebrews 11v22
Joseph was sure that God would bring the Israelites back out of Egypt. He told his family to carry his body back to Canaan with them.
"By faith Joseph gave instructions about his b_____." (v22)

17 ☐ Read Hebrews 11v23
The king of Egypt ordered that all Israelite baby boys were to be drowned. But Moses' parents hid him—and trusted God.
"By faith Moses' parents hid him for t _ _ _ _ months." (v23)

18 ☐ Read Hebrews 11v24-27
Moses was brought up by Pharaoh's daughter. But instead of living as an Egyptian, he became the leader of the Israelites and trusted God in the face of suffering.
"By faith Moses r _ _ _ _ _ _ to be known as the son of Pharaoh's daughter." (v24)

19 ☐ Read Hebrews 11v28
The Passover was the last of the ten plagues. The Israelites sprinkled blood on their doors and trusted God to keep their children safe.
"By faith Moses kept the P _ _ _ _ _ _ _ and the sprinkling of blood." (v28)

20 ☐ Read Hebrews 11v29
God made a dry path through the Red Sea to rescue the Israelites from the Egyptian army.
"By faith the people crossed the Red Sea as if on d _ _ land." (v29)

Extra Readings

21 ☐ Read Hebrews 11v30

Joshua led the Israelites into Canaan. Their first battle was for the city of Jericho. God won the battle for them!

"By faith the W _ _ _ _ of Jericho fell." (v30)

22 ☐ Read Hebrews 11v31

Rahab lived in Jericho—but she believed that God would give victory to the Israelites, so she helped Joshua's spies.

"It was faith that kept R _ _ _ _ from being killed." (v31)

23 ☐ Read Hebrews 11v32-38

These verses list many other people of faith. One is probably Daniel, who trusted and obeyed God, even when faced by hungry lions!

"---they shut the mouths of l _ _ _ _." (v33)

24 ☐ Read Hebrews 11v39-40

These people all trusted God—even though they didn't see all of the answers to God's promises.

"These were all commended for their f _ _ _ _." (v39)

25 ☐ Read Hebrews 12v1

Having read about so many people of faith, what should we do? Keep going! And keep trusting!

"Let us run with determination the r _ _ _ that lies before us." (v1)

26 ☐ Read Hebrews 12v2-3

Think about Jesus—He died for us and rose again. He has done everything for us. So keep on following and trusting Him. Don't give up!

"Let us keep our eyes fixed on J _ _ _ _ ." (v2)

WHAT NEXT?

We hope that **Table Talk** has helped you get into a regular habit of reading the Bible with your children.

Table Talk comes out every three months. Each issue contains 65 full **Table Talk** outlines, plus 26 days of extra readings. By the time you've used them all, the next issue will be available.

Available from your local Christian bookshop—or call us on **020 8942 0880** to order a copy.

COMING SOON!
Issue Four of Table Talk

Issue Four of Table Talk finishes the books of Matthew, Exodus and Acts. It dips into some of Paul's letters as well.

- Investigate the very first Easter in **Matthew's** Gospel.
- Wander through the wilderness with the Israelites in **Exodus**.
- Join Paul as he travels to Rome in **Acts**, and writes to some of the people he visited on his journeys.